SEAL HUNTER
IN THE
BERING SEA
(1893)

WAR CORRESPONDENT
IN KOREA AND JAPAN
(1904)

VOYAGE OF
THE *SNARK*
IN MELANESIA
(1908)

LIVING IN AUSTRALIA
AND TASMANIA
(1908–1909)

THE LIVES OF JACK LONDON

MICHEL VIOTTE

WITH NOËL MAUBERRET

TRANSLATED FROM FRENCH BY:
JACQUELINE DINSMORE

FIREFLY BOOKS

A FIREFLY BOOK

Published by Firefly Books Ltd. 2018

First printing

Publisher Cataloging-in-Publication Data (U.S.)

Library of Congress Control Number: 2018935544

Library and Archives Canada Cataloguing in Publication

Viotte, Michel
[Vies de Jack London. English]
     The lives of Jack London / Michel Viotte with Noël
Mauberret ; translated from the French by Jacqueline Dinsmore.
Translation of: Les vies de Jack London.
Includes index.
ISBN 978-0-228-10124-6 (hardcover)
     1. London, Jack, 1876-1916. 2. Authors, American--20th
century--Biography. I. Mauberret, Noël, author II. Dinsmore,
Jacqueline, 1951-, translator III. Title. IV. Title: Vies de Jack
London. English
PS3523.O46 Z99313 2018   813'.52   C2018-901310-9

Published in the United States by
Firefly Books (U.S.) Inc.
P.O. Box 1338, Ellicott Station
Buffalo, New York 14205

Published in Canada by
Firefly Books Ltd.
50 Staples Avenue, Unit 1
Richmond Hill, Ontario L4B 0A7

Translator: Jacqueline Dinsmore

Printed in China

ACKNOWLEDGMENTS

Alain Wieder, Jeanne Campbell Reesman, Sara S.
Hodson, Carol Dodge, Joe Lawrence, Rudy Cuica, Alain
Sprauel.

CONTENTS

↑
The painter Xavier Martinez
works on a portrait of his friend
Jack London. Wake Robin
Lodge, 1905. This painting
disappeared in the 1906 San
Francisco earthquake.

A SUPERB METEOR

"Every day I thought of going out beyond the sky-line to see the world."[1]

Jack London (1876-1916), author of *The Call of the Wild*, *White Fang* and *Martin Eden*, was the best-known American writer of his time. Drawing the material for his books from his tumultuous life, he embodied the very archetype of adventure at the turn of the 19th century.

He spent his early years haunted by the desire to succeed, and throughout his life was driven by the need to explore, discover, experience. In turn a vagabond, gold panner in the far north wilderness and sailor-explorer in the Polynesia and Melanesia archipelagos, he was also a rancher, war correspondent and passionate socialist activist.

Born when the conquest of the West was drawing to an end, he led life at a furious pace, accompanying the momentous changes of an America that was entering its modern era. Both his career and his work—unique, inextricable—are striking for their intensity. All his work seems to question our survival, whether in wild and hostile nature or in the so-called "civilized" capitalist world, ruthlessly exploiting the weakest and most destitute.

When he passed away at the age of 40, Jack London had become the most widely read author in the world, leaving behind more than fifty books, as well as dozens of press articles and thousands of photographs. Even today, he remains a formidable source of inspiration, a model of will and courage that ideally defines this "creed," reported by a journalist shortly before his death:

"I would rather be a superb meteor, every atom of me in magnificent glow, than a sleepy and permanent planet. The proper function of man is to live, not to exist. I shall not waste my days in trying to prolong them. I shall use my time." [2]

↑
Jack London, 1909.

→
Jack London photographed in the studio of Arnold Genthe, between 1900 and 1902.

"Jack London had a poignantly sensitive face. His eyes were the eyes of a dreamer, and there was an almost feminine wistfulness about him. And yet at the same time he gave the feeling of a terrible and unconquerable physical force" (Arnold Genthe).[3]

Next double page:

Jack London on his boat *Roamer*, between 1910 and 1913.

1876 — 1893

SAN FRANCISCO BAY

Jack London's time was that of the New America, forging a path of industrialization and technical progress. When he was born on January 12, 1876, the United States was just 100 years old.

That same year, General Custer's 7th Cavalry Regiment was overpowered by a coalition of Sioux and Cheyenne at the Battle of Little Big Horn, and Wild Bill Hickcok was shot dead in a saloon in Deadwood, Dakota. The taming of the West was drawing to a close: soon, all the Indians would be on reserves and the most famous survivors of these heroic times would end their lives in travelling shows like Buffalo Bill's *Wild West* show.

Millions of new immigrants from Europe were streaming into the country, and major cities like New York, Boston and Chicago were experiencing unprecedented growth. Imposing skyscrapers and electric streetcars defined new urban landscapes and, simultaneously, new railway lines were being completed throughout the country, allowing unhindered circulation of goods and people.

"My environment was crude and rough and raw. I had no outlook, but an uplook rather. My place in society was at the bottom. Here life offered nothing but sordidness and wretchedness, both of the flesh and the spirit; for here flesh and spirit were alike starved and tormented."[1]

←
Port of San Francisco,
late 19th century.

↑
Oakland Street,
late 19th century.

This tremendous expansion made the fortunes of large trusts and financial groups but plunged millions of Americans into poverty. Exploited by the system, they bore the brunt of the repercussions from several stock market crashes.

Jack grew up on the West Coast, in the slums of San Francisco. California was admitted as the 31st state soon after the Great Gold Rush of 1849, and its economic capital, San Francisco, immediately attracted scores of investors and adventurers. In just 20 years, the population of the city had quadrupled. For many newcomers, hard hit by the crash that shook the country, the California dream had turned into a nightmare.

Jack never knew his real father, who left the family before baby Jack was born. His mother, Flora, then married John London, a widower with two children who recognized Jack as his own son and gave him his name. John London worked as a carpenter, but his health suffered as a result of an injury sustained during the American Civil War. Flora was from a wealthy family in Ohio. She took in sewing work and gave piano lessons, dreaming of regaining her former status. She was also passionate about astrology and spiritualism, and was known for making tables shake and telling fortunes. She was a difficult, unpredictable woman. She was always very hard on Jack, rarely demonstrating her affection. It is with his adoptive father and stepsister Eliza that he would find tenderness and understanding, as well as with his "mammy," Jennie Prentiss, a former black slave who would remain close to him for many years.

←
Jack at the age of nine.

↗
Jack's class photo at Cole Grammar School in Oakland, 1887.

→
First known photo of Jack London.

Flora London

Flora London remained scarred for life because of a case of typhoid that struck her at the age of 13: her growth stopped—she was a little under five feet tall—and she lost all her hair. She hid her baldness with a wig.

In 1874, she moved to San Francisco with her companion, William Chaney, an astrologer whose lectures had had some success. A year later, when she announced that she was pregnant, he rejected any suggestion of paternity.

After many violent arguments, he left the city and abandoned her as she waited for the birth of her child. On September 7, 1876, she finally married John London; Jack was six months old.

Flora was an unstable and angry woman. She was sometimes described as overly dramatic, indulging in endless sessions of spiritualism during which she channeled an Indian chief named "Plume." She was often cold and authoritarian with Jack. However, all his life he would make sure that her needs were met, providing her with housing and financial support.

↑
Flora London
(1848-1922), née Wellman,
Jack London's mother.

John Griffith London
(1828–1887), Jack London's
adoptive father.

Eliza Shepard (1866–1939),
née London, daughter of John
London, and Jack's favorite
stepsister.

To overcome the financial difficulties at home, John London was constantly trying new occupations: grocer, market gardener, farmer, watchman and even railway worker. The family was forced to change addresses many times, first in San Francisco, then in the surrounding Bay areas of Oakland, Alameda or San Mateo County. Left to his own devices, Jack spent a lot of time walking the streets. Reading was often his only escape, and he devoured adventure novels and travel stories that he borrowed from the Oakland Public Library.

But as he grew older, Jack had less time to indulge in his passion for books. Flora soon compelled him to contribute to the family finances. From the age of ten, he worked numerous odd jobs: selling newspapers, delivering ice, sweeping saloons.

"But many a night I did not knock off work until midnight,"

"I read in bed, I read at table, I read as I walked to and from school, and I read at recess while the other boys were playing."[2]

↖
Vallejo Street Wharf, San Francisco, early 20th century.

↗
Southern Pacific's Oakland Long Wharf, early 20th century.

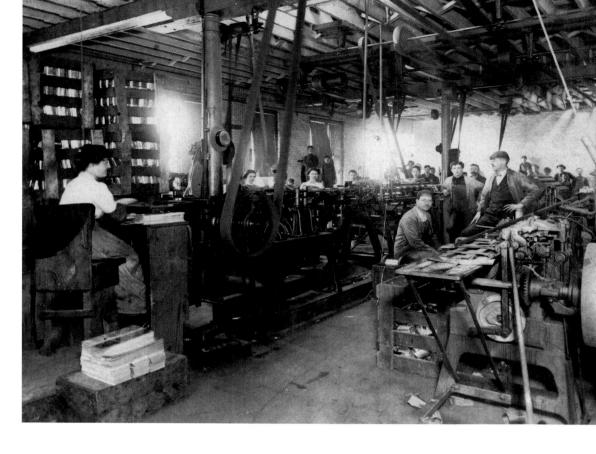

he later wrote. "On occasion I worked eighteen and twenty hours on a stretch. Once I worked at my machine for thirty-six consecutive hours."[4]

It would be on the Oakland docks, just steps from the cannery, that Jack escaped this suffocating atmosphere.

Fishing with John London, from the Alameda jetty or aboard a small boat, gave him a taste for the sea from a very young age. This is where he felt at home, with the sailors, stevedores and street vendors. He stared enviously at the oyster pirates who raided the bay, and whose exploits filled his dreams. At that point in time, the railroads and oyster companies exerted a virtual monopoly over the oyster trade, and the pirates would descend during the night to raid the beds and then sell their take on the black market the next morning.

↑
The Hickmott Cannery in Oakland, early 20th century. Jack worked there in the fall of 1889.

Next double page: Mission Street Wharf, San Francisco, late 19th century.

"And if a man is a born sailor, and has gone to the school of the sea, never in all his life can he get away from the sea again. The salt of it is in his bones as well as his nostrils, and the sea will call to him until he dies."[3]

It was risky business, but the profits justified the hazards: in one night they earned the equivalent of a worker's monthly salary. Jack did not hesitate for long: "I wanted to be where the winds of adventure blew. The penalty was State imprisonment, the stripes and the lockstep. And what of that? The men in stripes worked a shorter day than I at my machine. And there was vastly more romance in being an oyster pirate or a convict than in being a machine slave."[6]

"This is my only hope of escaping," he says to Jennie Prentiss, his former nanny. "I feel myself dying inside. I know I'm only fifteen, but I am strong and as tough as any of those oyster pirates."[7] London convinced his "mammy" to lend him $300, and bought his own boat, the *Razzle Dazzle*. He quickly won the respect of the Bay tough guys, like Whiskey Bob and Big Alec, and was soon dubbed "Prince of the Oyster Pirates."

Finally, an exciting life! He had to escape vigilantes' bullets, rival pirates, the fishing patrol: "There it was, the smack and slap of the spirit of revolt, of adventure, of romance, of the things forbidden and done defiantly and grandly. And I knew that on the morrow I would not go back to my machine."[8] The money he earned was soon spent freely in countless saloons, where an atmosphere of adventure and companionship reigned. Jack got drunk regularly, and Johnny Heinold's First and Last Chance Saloon on the waterfront became his second home: "I practically lived in saloons; became a bar-room loafer, and worse."[9]

When *Razzle Dazzle* was destroyed in a fire, he joined forces with "Young Scratch" Nelson, an illiterate giant whose ferocity was feared throughout the Bay, and with whom

"When I was sixteen I had already earned the title of 'prince.' But this title was given me by a gang of cut-throats and thieves, by whom I was called 'The Prince of the Oyster Pirates.' "[5]

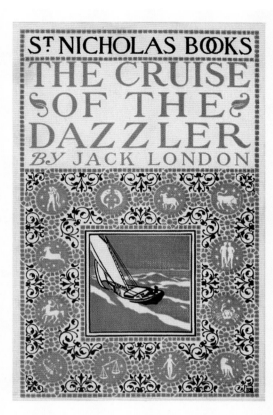

The Cruise of The Dazzler

Jack's experience with the Bay oyster pirates in 1891 was the inspiration for his first novel, *The Cruise of the Dazzler*, prepublished in *St. Nicholas Magazine* in July 1902 with the book appearing in October of the same year.

Joe, a young runaway, now denizen of San Francisco, signs on with French Pete's oyster pirate boat, the *Dazzler*. There he meets a young sailor his own age, Frisco Kid, an orphan from the mean streets, a real Jack London clone. The two boys become fast friends and share many wild and dangerous adventures. But Frisco Kid, who has known only detention centers all his life, dreams of escaping from his situation and getting an education.

Joe shows Frisco Kid the sordid side of their existence and persuades him to return with him to rejoin his family. Joe's family, grateful to have their son home, welcomes the Kid and gives him the life he had dreamed of.

←
Johnny Heinold behind his counter at the First and Last Chance Saloon on the Oakland docks, where Jack would get drunk with the other sailors.

↑
San Francisco Bay, late 19th century.

he continued to plunder the beds. But he gradually understood that this way of life could not last forever and ended up accepting a job with the Benicia Fish Patrol in early 1892.

The men on the fishing patrol were more bounty hunters than real police officers. Jack did not receive a salary, and was compensated through the fines imposed on the fishermen he helped arrest. Although he was on the other side of the fence, he continued to hang out on the docks, fighting and getting drunk with the other sailors. One night, while trying to board a boat to spend the night, he fell into the water, dead drunk. He gave in to the temptation to let himself drift and floated for four hours before recovering his wits and realizing that he did not want to die. Exhausted, he narrowly escaped drowning, thanks to the intervention of a Greek sailor who managed to fish him out.

He was not yet 17, but was ready to experience all the excesses, take all the risks. During the summer, while sailing in the Sacramento area, he met a gang of teenagers who hung out along the railroad tracks. Rebelling against all authority, these hardened kids lived by robbing and begging, and stowed away on freight trains, hanging under the cars. Seduced by this new challenge, Jack decided to take on the dangers of "the road." During a trip to Sierra Nevada, he also became one of the train hobos, and won a new nickname for his courage: Frisco Kid.

When he returned to San Francisco Bay, he felt ready to face the open sea. On January 20, 1893, he signed on as a common sailor aboard a three-master, the *Sophia Sutherland*, for a season of seal hunting off the coast of Japan.

On board the *Sophia Sutherland*, Jack was exposed to the traditional bullying of hardened sailors and had to once again take drastic measures to survive: "I had never

↓
Fisherman's Wharf, San Francisco, late 19th century.

been to sea before . . . It was either a case of holding my own with them or of going under. I had signed on as an equal, and as an equal I must maintain myself, or else endure seven months of hell at their hands."[10] The Pacific crossing lasted 51 days, during which he worked diligently and perfected his navigation skills. When the schooner was caught in a typhoon, he remained alone at the helm for nearly 40 minutes: the typhoon "seemed to stand up against you like a wall, making it almost impossible to move on the heaving decks or to breathe as the fierce gusts came dashing by. . . . The force of the wind filled the air with fine spray, which flew as high as the crosstrees and cut the face like a knife, making

↑
Fisherman's Wharf,
San Francisco,
late 19th century.

←
Jack at 17, sailor on the
Sophia Sutherland.

→
The *Sophia Sutherland*, aboard
which Jack embarked for a
seal-hunting season in the
Bering Sea in 1893.

it impossible to see over a hundred yards ahead. The sea was a dark lead color as with long, slow, majestic roll it was heaped up by the wind into liquid mountains of foam."[11] For the adventure-loving teenager, it was an experience that would never be forgotten.

After a stop at the Bonin Islands southeast of Japan, the *Sophia Sutherland* sailed north to the Bering Sea and began the hunt. For more than three months, the frozen bridge of the ship turned into a veritable slaughterhouse: as soon as they were caught, the seals were hoisted on board, where the crew dismembered their bloodied remains before throwing the carcasses back into the sea.

Jack returned to Oakland on August 26, 1893, to discover that many of his old friends had disappeared, often from violent deaths. Under the urging of his mother, he wrote a 2,000-word novel inspired by his trip for a contest in *The San Francisco Morning Call*. He won first prize, and his story, "Typhoon Off the Coast of Japan," appeared in the November 12th issue. Jack London's first published text earned him $25.

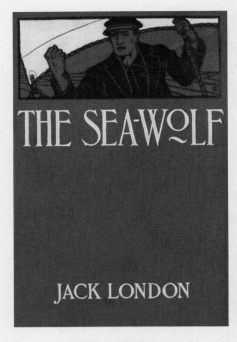

THE SEA-WOLF

JACK LONDON

The Sea-Wolf

Jack would detail his adventures on board the *Sophia Sutherland* in an autobiographical text: *That Dead Men Rise Up Never*. Discovered after his death, it would eventually be published in *The Human Drift* (New York, The Macmillan Co., 1917). But this chapter of his life was particularly significant in one of his major works of fiction: *The Sea Wolf* (pre-publication in *The Century Magazine* in January 1904 with the book released in October of the same year).

The story takes place largely aboard the *Ghost*, a schooner similar to the *Sophia Sutherland*, that also took part in the North Pacific seal hunt. It brings into conflict two opposing characters: the violent Captain Wolf Larsen, who believes only in strength and individualism; and the rich and cultured Humphrey van Weyden, shipwrecked and taken on board, defender of the values of tolerance and solidarity. Two visions of the world clash in the pages of the book, leaving no doubt on the complex personality of the author.

←
Illustration by W. J. Aylward for the prepublication of "The Sea Wolf" in *The Century Magazine*.

Tales of the Fish Patrol

Jack's real-life adventures in the Benicia Fish Patrol, straddling the line between fiction and autobiography, are related in a collection of short stories called *Tales of the Fish Patrol* (prepublished in *The Youth's Companion* magazine in February 1905, released in book form in September of the same year).

Jack describes in great detail the fishing methods, tricks used by poachers to evade the police and the clashes between rival Chinese, Greek and Italian crews. He presents captivating portraits of famous Bay characters, such as Big Alec or "The King of the Greeks," and the Chinese man, Yellow Handkerchief.

Prepublication of "Tales of the Fish Patrol" in *The Youth's Companion*, April 13, 1905.

CONFRONTING

UNRESTRAINED CAPITALISM

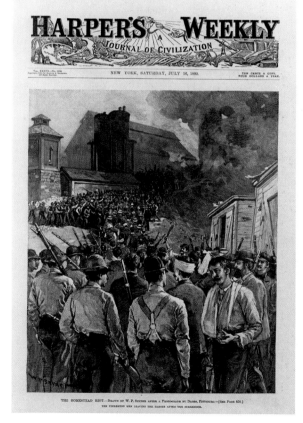

fter months on board the *Sophia Sutherland*, Jack learned that the health of John London, his adoptive father, had deteriorated further. The elder London's veteran's pension was no longer sufficient to support the family, and Jack had to quickly find a new job to support the household. He had no choice but to start again at the bottom of the ladder, with the hope, through sheer will and hard work, of changing his situation. He was hired by a jute mill, where he worked on the assembly line 10 hours a day, six days a week, for 10 cents an hour. He stayed there for several months, but eventually resigned when his bosses reneged on their initial promise to give him a raise. He then managed to get into the Oakland Power Plant, where he worked shoveling coal to power the boilers. But, again, he chose to leave when he learned that he had, by himself, replaced two recently dismissed men, one of whom had committed suicide.

← Jack London.

← Clash between hired guards, known as Pinkertons, and labor protestors at the Homestead steel mill. *Harper's Weekly*, July 16, 1892 (engraving by W. P. Snyder).

↓ Anti-Chinese riot in Denver, October 31, 1880.

While struggling to find a new job, a disgusted Jack realized he was trapped in a system of unrestrained capitalism that, buttressed by corrupt political power, had turned millions of Americans into true slaves. Social tensions in the country were at their height. Strikes proliferated and were severely repressed by authorities, as with the 1886 Haymarket riot in Chicago, when police charged demonstrators, killing one and wounding a dozen. To keep their businesses running, the bosses often resorted to using foreign laborers, who were more compliant. There followed a sharp rise in xenophobia, particularly on the West Coast, where Asian communities were subject to violent racism. Despite the adoption of the 1882 Chinese Exclusion Act, which brought all new immigration to a halt for a time, riots continued to erupt in Los Angeles, Seattle and Tacoma. Chinese immigrants saw their property ransacked and some were even forcibly removed from their homes. Jack's writings would later show the spirit of this period clearly, as, for example, in *Tales of the Fish Patrol*, where he regularly described the Chinese as being lustful and leering.

"Why is it that millions of modern men live more miserably than lived the caveman?"[1]

↑
Demonstration of the unemployed, New York, 1909.

←
First publication of the short story "The Apostate," in which Jack London denounces the exploitation of children by factory owners. *Woman's Home Companion*, September 1906.

→
Jack London.

A new financial crisis in 1893 caused the bankruptcy of many small businesses and farms, further aggravating the situation and plunging the country into the worst depression of its young history. America now had two million seasonal and unemployed workers.

"The Road had gripped me and would not let me go."[2]

It was at this point that Jacob Coxey, an industrialist from Ohio, organized a protest march of unprecedented scale. A true army made up of the unemployed from all over America headed for Washington to demand immediate action. Jack decided to join the West Coast contingent, about six hundred men, commanded by "General" Charles T. Kelly.

He missed their departure, though, and had to catch up. In a return to his time as the Frisco Kid, when he was hanging out with the Sacramento teenage gang, he stowed away on freight trains, crossing California, Nevada and Utah. He managed to join the group in the Rocky Mountains, near Laramie.

He continued with them eastward, through Wyoming, Nebraska and Iowa. The men traveled crowded into cattle cars put at their disposal by the railway companies, then had to continue on foot when access to trains was eventually disallowed. Their numbers increased unremittingly, and Kelly's army soon numbered 2,000. Along the way, expressions of solidarity and support were numerous: "The hospitable Iowa farmer-folk . . . turned out with their wagons and carried our baggage," remembered Jack. "[They] gave us hot lunches at noon by the wayside; mayors of comfortable little towns made speeches of welcome and hastened us on our way; deputations of little girls and maidens came out to meet us, and the good citizens turned out by hundreds, locked arms, and marched with us down their main streets. It was circus day when we came to town, and every day was circus day, for there were many towns. In the evenings our camps were invaded by whole populations."[5]

In Iowa, they eventually had to build flat-bottomed boats to continue their advance using the Des Moines River and the

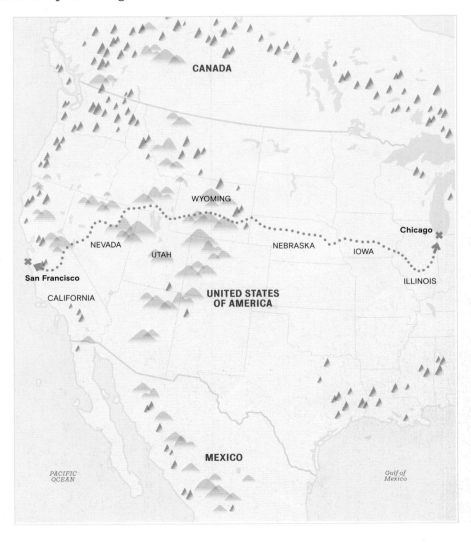

↑
Coxey's Army of unemployed
workers marches in Massillon,
Ohio, March 25, 1894.

←
Unemployed workers in
Coxey's Army marching on
Washington, 1894.

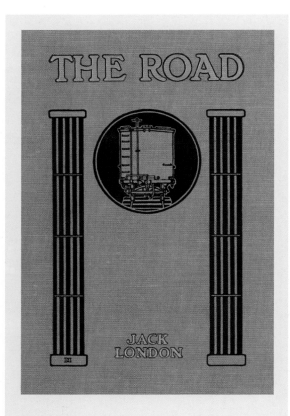

The Road

The collection *The Road* (prepublished in *Cosmopolitan* and published in book form in 1907) brings together nine autobiographical stories, in which Jack recounts his vagabond odyssey on the roads of the United States and Canada in 1894: his training with Kelly's Army of unemployed, his harsh detention in Erie County Penitentiary and his journey across Canada. Above all, he remembers with passion the feeling of freedom when he "rode the rods"[3] by traveling illicitly on railcar bogies, under the train cars, in spite of the danger: "In Hobo Land the face of life is protean—an ever changing phantasmagoria, where the impossible happens and the unexpected jumps out of the bushes at every turn of the road."[4]

↑
"General" Charles T. Kelly, leader of the Army of unemployed.

Mississippi. But in May, the announcement of the arrest of Coxey and his men in Washington, in front of the Capitol, was a fatal blow to the troop's morale, already struck low by heavy rains and lack of food. Discipline quickly disintegrated and, in Hannibal, Missouri, Jack gave up.

A penniless Jack resumed his hobo life. He traveled north through Ohio and Illinois, stayed in Chicago for a while, then decided to go to Niagara Falls. On June 28, in the city of Niagara Falls, he was arrested for vagrancy and sentenced to thirty days in jail. While incarcerated in Buffalo's Erie County Penitentiary, he found himself in the ideal position to evaluate the terrible living conditions in American prisons: "Our hall was a common stews, filled with the

↑
"General" Kelly's men, 1894.
Bottom right: Jack London?

ruck and the filth, the scum and dregs, of society—hereditary inefficients, degenerates, wrecks, lunatics, addled intelligences, epileptics, monsters, weaklings, in short, a very nightmare of humanity."[6] The memory of this experience would haunt him for many years.

Upon his release, he decided to see the big cities of the East before returning to California. He visited Washington, Baltimore, New York and Boston. As autumn arrived, he reached Montreal and crossed Canada, from east to west, by train, a distance of over two thousand miles. He made the trip illicitly aboard a cattle car, and along the way fraternized with many other wretched drifters: "I found there all sorts of men . . . sailor-men, soldier-men, labor-men, all wrenched and distorted and twisted out of shape by toil and hardship and accident, and cast adrift by their masters like so many old horses . . . I saw the picture of the Social Pit as vividly as though it were a concrete thing . . . And I confess a terror seized me."[8]

Back on the Pacific coast in Vancouver, he embarked on a steamship to Oakland, determined to give a new impetus to his life.

To break out of this vicious circle and move forward from his current situation, Jack realized there was only one solution: culture and

"I had been born in the working-class, and I was now, at the age of eighteen, beneath the point at which I had started. I was down in the cellar of society, down in the subterranean depths of misery."[7]

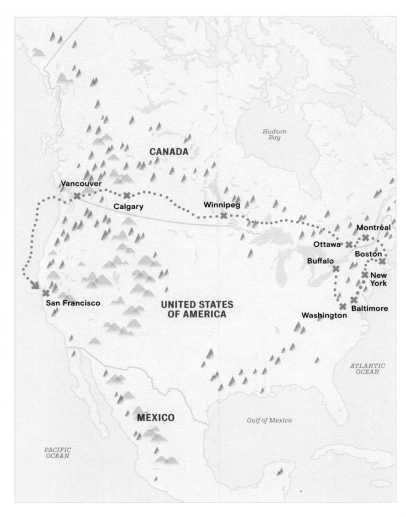

education. He decided to go back to school and acquire the basics needed if he were to become a writer.

He enrolled in Oakland High School, where the students in his class were all five years younger than he was. To pay for his classes and help his parents out financially, he worked for the school's cleaning service and swept the school rooms after classes. He worked tirelessly and visited the Oakland Public Library on a regular basis. At home, he spent his time studying and reading. He calculated how much sleep he needed: Two hours? Three? Four? Five? This would remain his routine for the rest of his life.

Reading the works of Karl Marx, Charles Darwin and Herbert Spencer was a revelation for Jack. He identified with their views, which awakened a new political awareness within him: "Other and greater minds, before I was born, had worked out all that I had thought and a vast deal more. I discovered that I was a socialist."[9]

In the second half of the 19th century, socialist ideas expanded throughout the United States, proliferated by the many European political refugees who arrived during that time. In 1872, New York became the seat of the Socialist International and in 1876, the first American organization, the Socialist Workers Party, was founded. Jack joined in April 1896, barely 20 years after its creation.

"I resolved to sell no more muscle, and to become a vendor of brains. Then began a frantic pursuit of knowledge."[10]

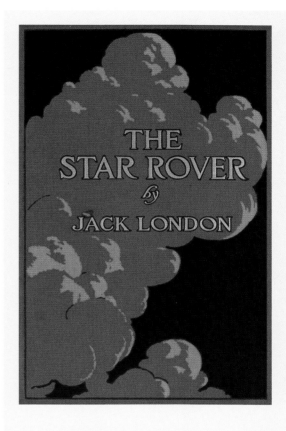

The Star Rover

Jack London's feelings of injustice and powerlessness towards the prison system that surfaced when he was incarcerated in Buffalo are dramatically reflected in the fantasy novel *The Star Rover* (prepublication in the *Los Angeles Examiner* and the *American Sunday Monthly Magazine* in February 1914, released in book form in 1915).

To survive the violence of the treatments he is subjected to, an unjustly sentenced prisoner, Darrell Standing, turns to self-hypnosis. He escapes through his mind, by projecting himself into past lives. He becomes, in turn, various imaginary characters: a 16th century French aristocrat, a Roman centurion, an English sailor. By freeing his mind from the grip of his captors this way, he is able, at the end of the book, to face his terrible punishment, for "Life is spirit, and spirit cannot die."[11]

He was frequently conspicuous for his incendiary anti-capitalistic remarks: "Arise, ye Americans, patriots and optimists! Awake! Seize the reins of a corrupt government and educate your masses!"[13]

Jack also spent a lot of time with the socialist speakers, perched on soapboxes in front of Oakland City Hall. His passionate speeches quickly earned him the nickname "Boy Socialist." The *San Francisco Chronicle*, on February 16, 1896, stated: "Jack London, who is known as the boy socialist of Oakland, is holding forth nightly to the crowds that throng City Hall Park. There are other speakers in plenty, but London always gets the biggest crowd and the most respectful attention."[14] His public pronouncements one day were even responsible for his arrest and brief imprisonment as an "agitator."

After Oakland High School, Jack enrolled at the Alameda Academy, which had a two-year program to prepare students for the UC Berkeley entrance exam. With fervid hard work, he absorbed the course material in four months and then successfully completed the tests. Johnny Heinold, owner of the First and Last Chance Saloon, loaned him the registration fee, and Jack walked onto the prestigious campus at the beginning of September 1896. He lasted only one semester, however—he felt out of touch with the other students, who he found immature and frivolous, the teaching too academic and ignoring the realities of the time. A disappointed Jack decided to put an end to boring studies that, in any case, he could no longer finance. On February 4, 1897, he left the university and began writing, focusing the whole might of his resolve on his task: "Early and late I was at it—writing, typing, studying grammar, studying writing and all the forms of writing, and studying the writers who succeeded in order to find out how they succeeded. At times I forgot to eat, or refused to tear myself away from my passionate outpouring in order to eat."[15]

"The revolution is here, now. Stop it who can."[12]

Jack London's Socialist Workers Party membership card, 1896.

Socialist Party of America poster for the presidential election, 1904.

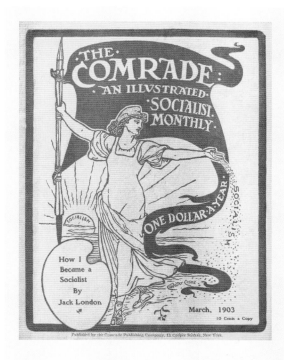

How I Became a Socialist

In March 1903, *The Comrade* published Jack's article "How I Became a Socialist" (reproduced in the collection *War of the Classes* in 1905), in which he explains how he became aware during his year spent on the road in 1894 of the state of deterioration of those around him, broken by drudgery and misery. He recognized the fate that awaited him and admitted that he was seized by a "terror."[17] After seeing the "walls of the Social Pit"[18] rising around him, he pledged never again to let himself be exploited by this capitalist system: ". . . and may God strike me dead if I do another day's hard work with my body!"[19]

But in order to eat, he had to find a job. He was hired to work in the laundry at Belmont Academy, a boarding school for upper-middle-class children. The work was exhausting, carried out in a veritable oven steeped in steam and detergents. And for thirty dollars a month! "So relentlessly did my partner and I spring into our work throughout the week that by Saturday night we were frazzled wrecks. I found myself in the old familiar work-beast condition."[16] Exhausted, Jack often thought of giving up his writing, and his dream of becoming a writer seemed to drift further away every day.

It was during this time, while busy researching at the San Francisco Library, that he discovered that his birth father was an astrologer named William Chaney. Jack managed to track him down and decided to contact him. Chaney, who was living on the East Coast, replied with a kind letter, but fiercely denied any question of paternity. Jack was 21, and this episode left him devastated.

1897 — 1902

ADVENTURES IN THE

FAR NORTH

O n July 14, 1897, the steamship *Excelsior* sailed into San Francisco. On board were 40 prospectors returning with $500,000 worth of gold from the Klondike, a wilderness area in western Canada. The news spread like wildfire and triggered an unprecedented stampede: in the following weeks, tens of thousands of men would set sail to take their chances in the North. They first had to travel to Alaska, a territory bought from Russia 30 years earlier—and then, from the cities of Juneau, Skagway or Dyea, complete a perilous journey of several hundred miles across the great expanses of the Far North before they could begin prospecting.

On July 25, Jack was one of the first to leave. He embarked on the SS *Umatilla* accompanied by his brother-in-law James Shepard, Eliza's husband. Once in Juneau, they hired the services of the Tlingit (the

← Prospectors' raft passing through the Miles Canyon Rapids, Yukon, 1898.

↑ The SS *Umatilla*, which carried Jack to the Klondike.

"The whole body of water, rushing crookedly into the narrow passage, accelerated its speed frightfully and was up-flung into huge waves, white and wrathful. This was the dread Mane of the White Horse."[1]

coastal peoples who guarded the Chilkoot Pass), and canoed up the Lynn Canal, then the Dyea River for 100 miles. Their first ordeal was Shepard's health; exhausted and sick, he had to return to Oakland. Jack then joined forces with some seasoned men he encountered along the way and set off to cross the terrifying Chilkoot Pass with the veterans.

The "Chilkoot," at 3,700 feet above sea level, offers the most direct passage between the mountains bordering Canada. To reach it, Klondikers had to climb one step at a time up a steep ice-covered slope, carrying all their equipment on their backs, an absolute nightmare. Their prospecting equipment, as well as warm clothes to survive in the arctic cold, tents, blankets and food, were separated into 65-pound loads. Each man then ferried these loads to the summit, walking in an unending column for days. Many men lost their lives in this ordeal, victims of exhaustion or carried away by avalanches.

Those who survived the Chilkoot Pass then had to follow the route to the lakes—Linderman, Bennett or Taggish—about 30 miles from there and build a raft to continue northwards down the Yukon River.

On September 8, Jack and his companions reached Linderman Lake and quickly set about building a small craft they called the *Yukon Belle*. With his maritime knowledge, Jack was promptly named captain. Then started a race against the clock to complete the journey before winter settled in and trapped the water in ice. Over a journey of more than 370 miles, the *Yukon Belle* faced frequent storms and extreme currents. It nearly capsized when passing through the White Horse or Box Canyon rapids. A month later, on October 9, the group finally reached a gold mining camp at Upper Island on the Stewart River and decided to move to nearby Henderson Creek to begin prospecting.

"They no longer walked upright under the sun, but stooped the body forward and bowed the head to the earth. Every back had become a pack-saddle."[2]

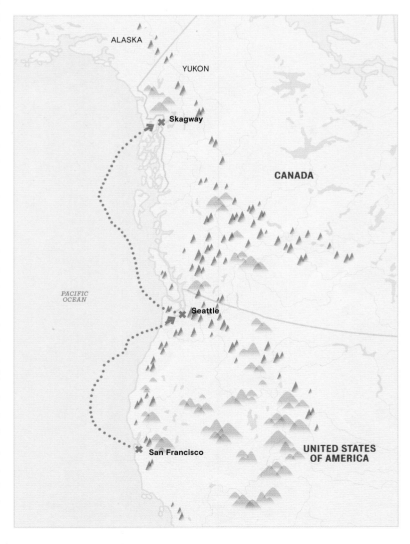

→
Californians on the deck of
the ship taking them from
San Francisco to the rich gold
fields of Alaska, 1897.

PORTAGE BETWEEN LAKES LINDERMAN AND BENNETT   1898

After a few days, Jack and three other companions had staked their spots and traveled to Dawson City, 80 miles to the north, to file their claims. Dawson was the only major town in the region, built from scratch in the early days of the rush and before long ballooned by thousands of newcomers. The Mounted Police patrolled the area, and in a few months, many shops and services appeared: a post office, bank, food stores, a church and a makeshift hospital built by a priest, Father William Judge. Above all, Dawson provided prospectors with the only recreation for miles around. The bars were open 24 hours a day and, for a little gold dust, provided alcohol, dancers and gambling. The White Chapel District offered several brothels and small wooden cabins where prostitutes entertained their clients.

Prospectors with their
dog team, Yukon, 1898.

At the beginning of December, after six weeks in Dawson, Jack returned to Henderson Creek with his registration in his pocket for Claim No. 54. Winter had fallen on the Yukon and made any attempt at prospecting impossible. Shut off in their isolated cabins, the gold seekers were forced to hang on for long months while enduring the glacial cold. Jack would later quip that a Klondike night equaled "forty days in a refrigerator."[4]

The ground inside was freezing and everyone needed to stay warmly dressed, moccasins on their feet. Their frozen food was stored on simple shelves. Jack spent long hours lying on his bunk, reading by the light of his kerosene lamp. He also enjoyed contemplating the surrounding wilderness, whose immutable calm impressed him: "Nature has many tricks wherewith she convinces man of his finity

↖
Prospectors preparing
to climb the Chilkoot Pass,
1898.

↑
Climbing the Chilkoot Pass,
1898

↑
Prospectors' boat, Yukon, 1897.

→
Cabin of Jack's friends, the
Bond brothers, Yukon, 1897.

. . . but the most tremendous, the most stupefying of all, is the passive phase of the White Silence. All movement ceases, the sky clears, the heavens are as brass; the slightest whisper seems sacrilege, and man becomes timid, affrighted at the sound of his own voice. Sole speck of life journeying across the ghostly wastes of a dead world, he trembles at his audacity, realizes that his is a maggot's life, nothing more. Strange thoughts arise unsummoned, and the mystery of all things strives for utterance. And the fear of death, of God, of the universe, comes over him, — the hope of the Resurrection and the Life, the yearning for immortality, the vain striving of the imprisoned essence, — it is then, if ever, man walks alone with God."[5] Jack would always regard the Far North as an exceptional revealer of human nature and explained that, in the Klondike, he had found himself.

"There nobody talks. Everybody thinks. You get your true perspective. I got mine."[3]

As proof, he took a knife and symbolically engraved on one of the walls of a friend's cabin: "Jack London, Miner, Author, Jan. 27, 1898."[6]

When he wanted to relieve his loneliness, Jack visited other nearby Klondikers for a drink and a few cigarettes, or a game of cards. Most of the time, their group could be found in French-Canadian Louis Savard's cabin, which was the roomiest and benefited from a large fireplace.

Discussions were lively around the fire and Jack often took the floor, developing his favorite themes: Darwin, Spencer and socialist ideology. Despite his young age—he was then only 21—he captivated this new audience and earned their respect: "One could not meet him without feeling the impact of a superior intellect,"[7] reported a friend.

They frequently shared their meals. The menu was nearly invariable: beans with bacon and a few slices of leavened bread, fried in a pan. A few times, a moose brought back from the hunt broke the routine.

When spring arrived, the melting of the snow mantle finally allowed prospecting to resume. But Jack's pickaxe failed to reveal the thinnest vein. It soon became clear that the Yukon would not turn out to be his hoped-for Eldorado. His inexperience was certainly a factor,

Burning Daylight

The first third of the novel *Burning Daylight* (prepublication in the *New York Herald* June 1910, book published in October of the same year), fashioned in the form of a fable, takes place in the expanses of the Far North during the gold rush. The main character, Elam Harnish, is a gold digger, nicknamed "Burning Daylight" for his energy and zeal for getting an early start to the day. He's a force of nature, famous throughout the Klondike, whose every visit to the Dawson City saloons became the stuff of legends.

After 12 years of prospecting, Elam finally discovers a rich vein. He heads back to California with his fortune to start a business where he must contend with the world of finance, again with success. But success leaves him with a bitter taste; disgusted by a corrupt and immoral system, he feels the need to find meaning for his life. When he discovers love, he decides to retire to his ranch and live simply, along with his beloved.

HOUSEKEEPING IN THE KLONDIKE

BY JACK LONDON

ILLUSTRATED BY E. W. DEMING

OUSEKEEPING in the Klondike—that's bad! And by *men* —worse. Reverse the proposition, if you will, yet you will fail to mitigate, even by a hair's-breadth, the woe of it. It is bad, unutterably bad, for a man to keep house, and it is equally bad to keep house in the Klondike. That's the sum and substance of it. Of course men will be men, and especially is this true of the kind who wander off to the frozen rim of the world. The glitter of gold is in their eyes, they are borne along by uplifting ambition, and in their hearts is a great disdain for everything in the culinary department save "grub." "Just so long as it's grub," they say, coming in off trail, gaunt and ravenous, "grub, and piping

"SARCASTIC COMMENTS ON THE WAY YOU FRY THE BACON."
Drawn by E. W. DEMING.

←
"Housekeeping in the Klondike."
Jack London's article describing
the lives of prospectors in the
Klondike, *Harper's Bazaar*,
September 15, 1900.

↓

Next double page:
Prospectors, 1898.

but the deterioration of his health was also a concern: he contracted scurvy, "Arctic leprosy," caused by lack of fresh vegetables in his diet. The disease was exhausting. His gums bled, his teeth came loose, his face swelled up. He was treated for several days at the hospital in Dawson, but his condition continued to decline. He had no other choice, if he wanted to survive, but to return to California as soon as possible.

On June 8, 1898, he embarked with two companions in a canoe and traveled 1,500 miles leaving the Yukon, north to the Arctic Circle, before bearing west to link up with the Bering Sea. After 20 days, he reached St. Michael, Alaska, a center of Inuit trade where a US military post had just been established. From there, he managed to get to Seattle on board a schooner before finally making his way to San Francisco by steamship.

Back in Oakland, Jack learned that John London, his adoptive father, had died during his absence. Although without resources, he alone was now responsible for taking care of his family's needs. The sale of his gold dust brought him $4.50 (!) and, although he quickly recovered from the scurvy, he was unable to find a job. So, he decided to plunge back into writing, with typical manic stubbornness.

He flooded editors and magazines with novels, articles, poems, songs and plays. He even had to borrow money for stamps, and pawned his few possessions: his watch, his bicycle, his raincoat. For months, his texts were regularly rejected. Yet he refused to despair, aware that his writing was gradually improving, and with the deep conviction that success awaited him at the end of the road: "I'm going to stick to my writing, and the publishers are going to accept it whether they like it or not. And some of these days they'll be glad to take the stuff they've rejected and pay me a good price for it. Some day I shall hit upon my magnum opus."[9]

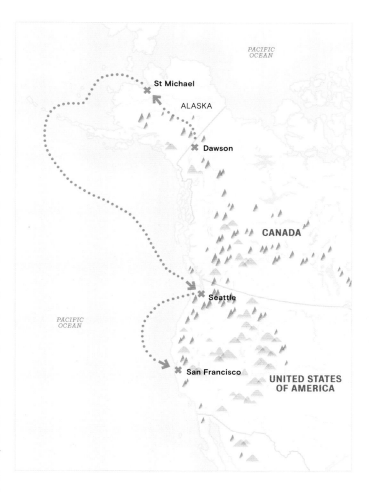

Smoke Bellew

Smoke Bellew, (prepublication in *Cosmopolitan* magazine in 1911, published in book form in October 1912) is Jack London's last work on the Far North. In it, he continued to describe the harsh living conditions in the Yukon, but this time in a quirky, humorous way. The collection includes 12 short stories, and its main character is Christopher Belliou, a San Francisco journalist, who set off on a gold rush adventure to find new literary inspiration.

Having sailed to Alaska on the SS *Excelsior*, he crosses the Chilkoot Pass, faces the rapids on the Yukon River and arrives in Dawson City, where he takes part in a sled race to win a valuable claim. These vagaries are all experienced with another prospector encountered along the way nicknamed "Shorty," because of his small size, and the two make a comical duo. Christopher also earns a nickname along the way, "Smoke Bellew," in reference to the speed he exhibits on the trail!

Dawson City street,
Yukon, 1899.

→
Some of Jack London's first
published stories: "The Son of
the Wolf," *Overland Monthly*,
April 1899; "Semper Idem," *The
Black Cat*, December 1900;
"Two Gold Bricks," *The Owl*,
September 1897.

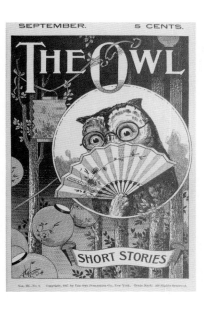

Jack drew tremendous literary inspiration from his adventures in the Far North and planned to transcribe what he experienced along with the many stories collected from other prospectors, trappers and Indigenous peoples: men fighting against the cold, the solitude, the wolves and, of course, the madness of the gold rush. Gradually, his efforts were rewarded. In January 1899, six months after his return, "To the Man on the Trail," one of his first short stories, appeared in the magazine *Overland Monthly*. He received five dollars in payment.

Others followed, in the space of a few months: "A Thousand Deaths," "In a Far Country," "From Dawson to the Sea," and on April 7, 1900, his first collection, *The Son of the Wolf*, was published. His second, *The God of His Fathers*, appeared the following year. Then a third, *Children of the Frost*, in 1902.

Jack's realistic style, stripped of all the artifice of 19th century Victorian literature, seduced readers and critics alike. In both New York and San Francisco, they could not stop singing his praises and started calling him the "Kipling of the North."

"A stream of short stories flowed from his pen."[8] (*Martin Eden*)

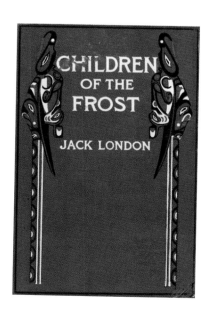

↑
Prospectors, 1898.

←
Some of Jack London's first published books: *The Son of the Wolf* (Boston: Houghton, Mifflin Co., 1900); *A Daughter of the Snows* (New York: J.B. Lippincott Co., 1902); *Children of the Frost* (New York: The Macmillan Co., 1902).

The White Man's Way

By JACK LONDON

T O cook by your fire and to sleep under your roof for the night," I had announced on entering old Ebbits' cabin; and he had looked at me blear eyed and vacuous, while Zilla had favored me with a sour face and a contemptuous grunt. Zilla was his wife, and no more bitter tongued, implacable old squaw dwelt on the Yukon. Nor would I have stopped there had my dogs been less tired or had the rest of the village been inhabited. But this cabin alone had I found occupied, and here, perforce, I took shelter.

Old Ebbits now and again pulled his tangled wits together, and hints and sparkles of intelligence came and went in his eyes. Several times in course of the preparation of my supper he even essayed hospitable inquiries about my health, the condition and number

these shall go into other mouths than thine and mine, old man."

Ebbits nodded his head and wept silently.

"There be no one to hunt meat for us!" she cried, turning fiercely upon me.

I shrugged my shoulders in token that I was not guilty of the unknown crime imputed to me.

"Know, oh white man, that it is because of thy kind, because of all white men, that my man and I have no meat in our old age and sit without tobacco in the cold."

"Nay," Ebbits said gravely, with a stricter sense of justice. "Wrong has been done us, it be true; but

lost. Does the white man like tobacco? I do not know. But if he likes tobacco, why does he spit out its value and lose it in the snow. It is a great foolishness and without understanding."

He ceased, puffed at the pipe, found that it was out, and passed it over to Zilla, who took the sneer at the white man off her lips in order to pucker them about the pipe stem. Ebbits seemed sinking back into his senility with the tale untold, and I demanded:

"What of thy sons Moklan and Bidarshik? And why is it that you and your old woman are without meat at the end of thy years?"

He roused himself as from sleep, and straightened up with an effort. "It is not good to steal," he said. "When the dog takes your meat you beat the dog with a club. Such is the law. It is the law the

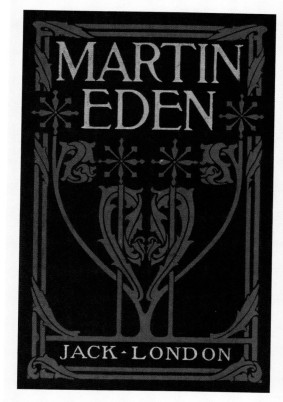

Martin Eden

"Yet I was Martin Eden."[10] Through the eponymous character of Martin Eden, protagonist of the novel (prepublication in The *Pacific Monthly* in September 1908, published in book form by Macmillan and Co. in 1909), Jack London tells a largely autobiographical story of his literary beginnings.

Without resources and with no education, Martin, a young sailor, has the fierce desire to climb out of his circumstances and take his place in society: "I will cover it if I have to do it on my hands and knees."[11] He decides to become a writer and gain fame and fortune to win the heart of a young woman from San Francisco's upper crust. He studies grammar, novels, theater, and poetry. He dissects the style of well-known authors, struggles "in the dark, without advice, without encouragement, and in the teeth of discouragement."[12] Martin suffers countless rejections, but with hard work, his realistic style— out of step with the literary tastes of his time— finally prevails and makes him a famous writer.

←
Prepublication of the short story "The White Man's Way" in the *New York Tribune* Sunday Magazine, November 4, 1906.

↑
Jack London.

No.19.

1902—1904

CELEBRATED

AUTHOR

As America entered the 20th century, Jack began a new life. He was now a well-known author, and his personal life, too, was radically altered. The very day his first book was published, he married Bessie Maddern, a close friend who had helped him prepare for the Berkeley University entrance examination. He was not really in love, but the two had formed a close bond. Bessie reviewed and retyped his manuscripts, and both enjoyed long bike rides and frequent picnics in the hills.

The couple moved to a big seven-room house in Oakland, and Jack organized his life in a predictably methodical way. Every day he sat at his desk and wrote at least a thousand words. He would not stray from this essential rule for the rest of his life. The rest of the time he spent in an assortment of physical activities: fencing, boxing, swimming, sailing and cycling. He also spent time with a new circle of friends, artists for the most part, including painter Xavier Martinez, photographer Arnold Genthe, drama critic Blanche Partington and poet George Sterling.

On January 15, 1901, the family expanded with the birth of a little girl, Joan.

←
Jack London.

↑
Jack and Bessie, 1902.

↑
Jack and Bessie, between 1900 and 1902.

←
Jack and Bessie's first house, 1130 East 15th Street, Oakland.

↑
Jack with Bessie (left) and
Mabel Applegarth (his first
great love, who was the
inspiration for Ruth Morse
in *Martin Eden*), San Jose,
July 1901..

Funds were now coming in regularly, but the expenses Jack had to face had become significant. He took on, of course, his own household expenses, but also those of his mother, Flora, and lent money to many of his friends. To balance his finances, he began writing numerous articles for newspapers and magazines in addition to his work as a fiction author.

At that time, the print media in the United States experienced unprecedented expansion. Whereas, in 1870, there were almost as many newspapers in the country as in the rest of the world, this number doubled in the space of ten years. And the phenomenon leaped forward again in 1885 with the invention of the linotype, which revolutionized the printing process. Until then, typesetters had to manually arrange text characters one by one to compose pages. The linotype allowed typesetters to directly type the words on a keyboard, in much less time, and so newspapers were able to significantly increase the number of pages they published. Newspaper owners built true empires based on prestigious titles with surprising print runs: Joseph Pulitzer owned the *New York World*; William Randolph Hearst the *New York Journal* and the *San Francisco Examiner*, Franck Munsey the *Washington Times;* and Adolph Ochs the *New York Times*. News agencies, such as the Associated Press and rival United Press, also opened their first offices abroad.

Working with major newspapers guaranteed Jack, whose writing was now appreciated, a significant increase to his income.

In 1902, the American Press Association asked Jack to go to South Africa, where the Boer War had just ended, to record the personal accounts of the British staff there. But as he was preparing to leave for a

The poor lining up at the Salvation Army in the East End, 1902 (photograph by Jack London).

Jack dressed as a penniless sailor to blend in with social rejects in London's East End, 1902.

stopover in Europe before heading to South Africa, he learned that his mission had been canceled, the officers having left African soil. He decided to use his ticket for England anyway, with the idea of writing a book about the abject neighborhood of London's East End. After convincing his New York publisher of the value of this new project, he embarked on a steamship for Liverpool and reached the capital in August 1902.

London's East End is situated northeast of the Thames. At the height of the city's boom in the early 19th century, downtrodden inhabitants and immigrants called the area home and still live there today, a great many of them still in extreme poverty. For his investigation, Jack chose to immerse himself in their lives, dressed in an old worn-out suit to pass as an American sailor.

↑
The poor lining up for food vouchers at the Salvation Army in East End London, 1902 (photograph by Jack London).

Christ Church, Spitalfields,
London, 1920 (photograph by
Jack London).

Misery in London's East End,
1902 (photograph by Jack
London).

→
"On the benches was arrayed
a mass of miserable and
distorted humanity . . .",
London's East End, 1902
(photograph by Jack London).

He shared their desperate lives for several months so he could render a fair account of their terrible living conditions. And what he discovered went beyond anything he could have imagined: crushed by the system, the poor lived in slums or lined up for hours at workhouses for a meal and a bed. The law prohibited sleeping outdoors, so when the shelters were full, society's outcasts had to walk the streets all night long, rummaging through garbage to survive, without ever a hope of finding a job.

Jack's observations were shocking: "East London is such a ghetto, where the rich and the powerful do not dwell, and the traveller cometh not, and where two million workers swarm, procreate, and die."[2]

"A pavement folk, as it were, lacking stamina and strength. The men become caricatures of what physical men ought to be, and

"Presto! in the twinkling of an eye, so to say, I had become one of them."[1]

↑
The Paris quays, 1902
(photograph by Jack London).

↑
Venice, 1902 (photograph by
Jack London).

their women and children are pale and anemic, with eyes ringed darkly, who stoop and slouch, and are early twisted out of all shapeliness and beauty . . . The men of the Ghetto are the men who are left, a deteriorated stock left to undergo still further deterioration."[3] The title of his book, *The People of the Abyss*, published the following year, leaves no doubt as to the situation.

"Nowhere in the streets of London may one escape the sight of abject poverty."[4]

Jack was keen to augment his impassioned writing by adding many of his own photographs that he took using a small, discreet camera. He had been extremely interested in this medium for some time and recent technological developments opened up a world of possibilities for him. Flexible filmstrips, invented by George Eastman, founder of Kodak, had gradually replaced the system of dangerous bulky photographic plates and, since 1898, new portable devices had appeared on the market. Jack had acquired a Kodak 3A which, once the bellows were folded, could be carried in a coat pocket. It would become an invaluable companion on all his travels.

Before returning to the United States, Jack decided to take a break playing tourist in Europe and crossed France and Italy by train. On October 20, 1902, when Becky, his second daughter, was born, he left for home. He arrived in New York on November 4, with a suitcase full of manuscripts and photographs.

Despite the arrival of the new baby, Jack and Bessie's relationship seemed at an impasse. Their relationship had actually started to deteriorate during the first year of their marriage. Bessie proved to be cold and without imagination, entirely dedicated to her role as a mother. Jack started seeing other women, among them Anna Strunsky, a young Jewish woman whose parents had fled Tsarist Russia. The two shared the same socialist convictions with a penchant for literature. In 1902, they wrote *The Kempton-Wace Letters* together, a work in the form of an exchange of correspondence questioning the very nature of love.

↓
Original cover of *The People of the Abyss*, New York, The Macmillan Co., 1903

↘
1908 advertisement for the Kodak 3A, the camera used by Jack London.

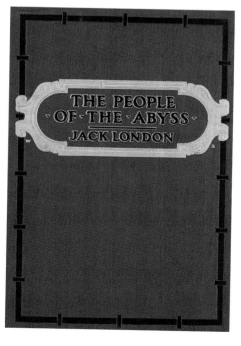

$20.00

Every feature that the expert requires in a hand camera—that simplicity which means so much to the beginner—these are in perfect combination in

The No. 3 A Folding POCKET KODAK

Broader in its scope than anything heretofore attained in pocket photography. Makes pictures 3¼ x 5½ inches, yet will go in an ordinary top-coat pocket. Loads in daylight with film cartridges for ten exposures, has a Double Combination Rapid Rectilinear lens of 6½ inch focus and a speed of f. 8, and the F. P. K. Automatic shutter for time, "bulb" or instantaneous exposures and fitted with iris diaphragm stops Nos. 4 to 128 inclusive. Rising, falling and sliding front, brilliant reversible finder, two tripod sockets and automatic focusing lock. Made of aluminum and covered with the finest seal grain leather. Perfect in every detail, and subjected to the most rigid inspection. Price, $20.00.

Kodak Catalog free at the dealers or by mail.

EASTMAN KODAK CO.
ROCHESTER, N. Y., *The Kodak City.*

↑
Jack with his two daughters,
Becky and Joan, 1906.

→
Original cover of *The
Kempton-Wace Letters* (The
Macmillan Co., 1903) written
by Jack with Anna Strunsky. In
the novel, the two characters
challenge each other's
contrasting visions of love:
the man defends a caring
relationship whose ultimate
goal is the procreation,
perpetuation and improvement
of the human species. But for
the woman, the grandeur and
beauty of love exists because
it has no room for reason.

→
Anna Strunsky.

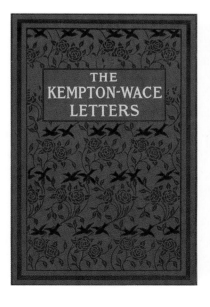

Jack was 26 years old when he returned from Europe. He was a warm, cultivated man, whose masculine good looks left no one indifferent. "He was youth, adventure, romance," Anna Strunsky would say a few years later. "He was a poet and a thinker. He had a genius for friendship. He loved greatly and was greatly loved."[5] The eager admirers who constantly surrounded him fed Bessie's jealousy and anger. To escape the oppressive atmosphere of his home, Jack bought a small boat, the *Spray*, which he sailed in the Bay and on neighboring rivers, sometimes alone, sometimes with friends. By the end of July 1903, he had made his decision: he announced to Bessie that he was going to leave her.

↑
Jack at the helm of the *Spray*, between 1903 and 1904.

↑
Jack London's *Spray* in San Francisco Bay, between 1903 and 1904.

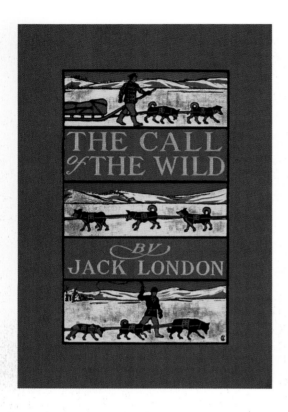

←
Original cover of *The Call of the Wild*, New York, The Macmillan Co., 1903. This work remains as its author's best-known work. *The Call of the Wild* has also been the subject of many screen adaptations, the most famous being William A. Wellman's (1935) with Clark Gable, and Ken Annakin's (1972) with Charlton Heston.

At that time, his career also took a new turn. On June 20, the serialized version of his latest Far North story, "The Call of the Wild," began in the *Saturday Evening Post*. The book came out a few weeks later. Although his first novel, *Daughter of the Snows*, had disappointed critics, this one would captivate them and turn the author's life upside down.

It tells the story of Buck, a dog that is stolen and shipped to the icy expanses of the Klondike at the time of the Gold Rush. Condemned to work as a sled dog, he must adapt to this new wild, hostile and dangerous environment to survive. When his new master disappears, his instinct drives him to leave the company of men and join a pack of wolves, his wild ancestors: "When the long winter nights come on and the wolves follow their meat into the home valleys, he may be seen running at the head of the pack through the pale moonlight or glimmering borealis leaping gigantic above his

"It had been discovered that he was a stylist, with meat under his style"[6] (*Martin Eden*).

→
Jack London.

THE OUTDOOR STORY NUMBER

THE SATURDAY EVENING POST

An Illustrated Weekly Magazine
Founded A°·D¹ 1728 *by* Benj.Franklin

JUNE 20, 1903   FIVE CENTS THE COPY

DRAWN BY CHARLES LIVINGSTON BULL

CHARLES LIVINGSTON BULL

Beginning The Call of the Wild—By Jack London

THE CURTIS PUBLISHING COMPANY, PHILADELPHIA

fellows, his great throat a-bellow as he sings a song of the younger world, which is the song of the pack."[7]

In this story, Buck embodies Jack. Through the dog's odyssey, Jack expresses his profound philosophy and the nightmares that haunt him: how he too had to fight to survive, and reinvent his life. And the figure of the wolf, now reproduced on the bookplate of all his works, became the symbol of Jack London, writer.

In the United States, *The Call of the Wild* was 1903's bestseller. Over the years, its success would endure, and millions of copies would be sold. This did not make the author wealthy: pressed by his debts, Jack had ceded the rights to his publisher for a lump sum of $2,000. No matter—the book made him a world-renowned star and had newspapers fighting over him.

← ↓
First installment of *The Call of the Wild*, serialized in the *Saturday Evening Post*, June 20, 1903.

↖
Jack London bookplate reproduced in all his works. The figure of the wolf became the hallmark of Jack London as a writer.

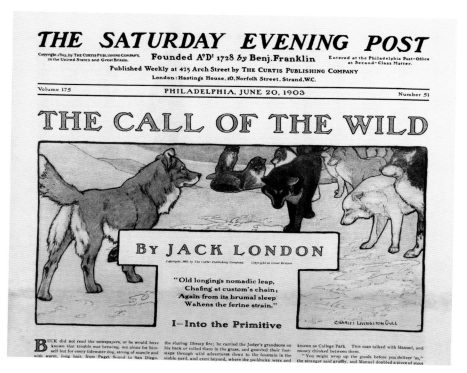

CORRE-SPONDENT

D espite his success, Jack continued to pursue ready money. His separation from Bessie had further increased his financial burden, and he now had to rent and maintain three homes: one for his mother, one for Bessie and two daughters and one for himself. Not to mention that he must also feed, dress and otherwise support his small clan. So, when press mogul William Randolph Hearst offered him a trip to Asia as a war correspondent to write a series of articles for the *San Francisco Examiner*, he jumped at the chance.

In February 1904, conflict broke out between Russia and Japan for control of Korea and Manchuria. The area contained significant mineral resources and provided strategic access to the Pacific Ocean, where the Russians planned on building a major railway line. After a surprise attack on the Russian naval base in Port Arthur, Manchuria, the Japanese Empire declared war on Nicholas II and launched a land campaign in Korea.

←
Jack being scrutinized by Japanese military, Korea, 1904.

↑
William Randolph Hearst, the giant American press magnate. Jack London contributed to several of his publications, including *The San Francisco Examiner*, *Collier's*, *Cosmopolitan* and *Harper's Bazaar*.

Jack London.

Crew and passengers on
the junk that took Jack up
the Korean coast toward
Chemulpo, 1904 (photograph
by Jack London).

↑
Jack in Korea, 1904.

↑
Inhabitants of Mokpo, Korea, 1904 (photograph by Jack London).

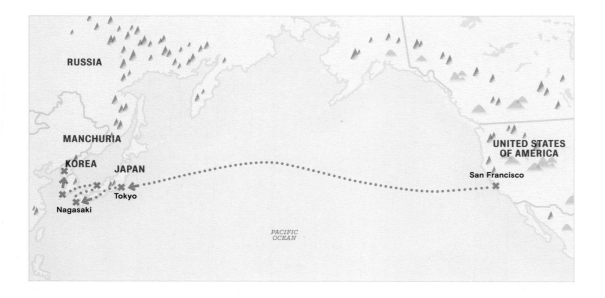

On January 7, 1904, Jack embarked on the SS *Siberia* bound for Yokohama. Arriving in Tokyo on January 24, he found himself held with the other correspondents by the Japanese authorities, who wanted to keep them away from the combat zones. Furious, he decided to reach the front secretly, using his own resources. He crossed Japan by rickshaw, then train and finally managed to be dropped by a steamship in Busan. From that point, he rented a junk and crew of three Koreans to travel up the coast, from the Sea of Japan to the China Sea. A wild storm broke the mast and rudder and, in Gunsan, Jack was forced to rent a new boat so he could carry on. Navigation was extremely difficult: temperatures were below zero, currents were strong and the crew worked steadily to circumvent rocky reefs. And all the while, the bridge was incessantly swept by icy waves. When he finally reached the city of Chemulpo, where the bulk of Japanese troops were based, Jack's fingers, ears and feet were frozen.

From Chemulpo, he hoped to return by land to the Chinese border. He encountered another American correspondent who arrived before the area was closed off by the Japanese authorities and decided to team

"Daily transports from Japan arrive, drop anchor in the outer harbor and men, horses, mountain artillery . . . depart by train to Seoul, twenty-seven miles away."[1]

↑
Jack in Korea, 1904.

→
Advance of Japanese troops
in Korea, 1904 (photograph by
Jack London).

Advance of Japanese troops in Korea, 1904 (photographs by Jack London).

↑
Korean refugees, 1904
(photograph by Jack London).

←
Port of An-Tung, Manchuria,
1904 (photograph by Jack
London).

←
War correspondents watching the Battle of the Yalu River, 1904 (photograph by Jack London).

Next double page: Port of An-Tung, Manchuria, 1904 (photograph by Jack London).

up with him. The men bought two saddle horses and three pack-horses, hired a Japanese interpreter, a cook and two Korean care-takers for the horses, and headed north. The roads were reserved for the army, so Jack's company had to make headway through ice-covered mountains and rice paddies. In Pyongyang, they were ordered to turn back. They continued nonetheless, but were eventually arrested in Sunan. After four days in jail, they were deported to Seoul, where authorities forced them to wait for other correspondents from Tokyo. A month later, on April 16, Jack finally managed to leave the city and reached the border of Manchuria on horseback. He got to the Chinese city of An-Tung, where Russian and Japanese forces were engaged in the first significant land battle of the First Sino-Japanese War, the Battle of the Yalu River. But Japanese military staff consigned journalists to an observation post, prepared especially for them, about forty miles away. Fed up, Jack ultimately accepted that access to the combat zones would be impossible.

Another incident precipitated the end of his Korean adventure. He surprised an officer's valet searching his belongings, looking for something to steal, and attacked him. He was arrested by the military police and was at risk of court-martial. President Theodore Roosevelt, informed by his consul in Tokyo, had to intervene personally to get Jack released. Jack was decisively expelled from the country in June.

"I've wasted 5 months of my life in this war,"[2] he later declared. Yet, with 19 articles filed, Jack

delivered the most comprehensive report on the first months of the conflict. He also presented, through hundreds of pictures, a critical photographic testimony of the Korean people's suffering. Above all, he helped Western readers become aware of the power of Japan's imperialism, and the organization and discipline of its then underrated army.

After Jack's departure, the Russo-Japanese War would continue for more than a year. Because of its length, the types of operations—by both naval and land forces—and the scale of the resources committed (more than two million men), it constituted the first major international conflict of the 20th century.

The Russo-Japanese peace treaty was signed on September 5, 1905, in Portsmouth, New Hampshire, where the Russian and

"I came to war expecting to get thrills. My only thrills have been those of indignation and irritation."[3]

↑
Jack writing one of his articles in his hotel room, Seoul, 1904.

→
Russian prisoners, 1904 (photograph by Jack London).

PROGRESS!
During the first Twenty-three Days of APRIL

"THE EXAMINER" Printed 30,152 *Inches* of Advertising A GAIN OF 2,655 Inches or 132⅓ Cols. over the corresponding time of April, 1903.

The San Francisco Examiner

AN AMERICAN PAPER FOR THE AMERICAN PEOPLE

THE WEATHER
Forecast made at San Francisco for 30 hours ending midnight April 25, 1904:
San Francisco and vicinity—Partly cloudy Monday; fresh southwest wind.
G. H. WILLSON, Local Forecaster.

VOL. LXXX.   MONDAY   SAN FRANCISCO, APRIL 25, 1904.   MONDAY   NO. 115.

JACK LONDON THE VICTIM OF JEALOUS CORRESPONDENTS

PUNISHED FOR ALERTNESS.—

On the protest of the discomfited and disgruntled war correspondents sitting around in remote Japanese towns, Jack London has been ordered back from the front. He was the only representative sent out by the American or British press who succeeded in getting close to the firing line. He was the only war correspondent who sent authentic news from the front, and he has sent the only real photographs from the seat of war.

Of course the exclusive matter sent by London to the Hearst newspapers raised a tremendous commotion in the home offices. Angry inquiries were sent out to the correspondents, complaining that they had allowed themselves to be beaten ignominiously. If London could get the real news what were they about? In this awkward predicament—awkward for the men who got left—the correspondents united in a tearful protest to the Japanese military censorship at Tokio, begging that London be recalled from Sunan, so as to save the reputation of the long lost correspondents. Their humble petition was granted. London was ordered back from Sunan to Seoul.

As a matter of fact, Jack London took serious risks in getting to the front and underwent severe hardships. He made his way north in an open boat with the thermometer fourteen degrees below zero at the risk of his life. The other correspondents for the most part sat around the clubs at Tokio and cultivated a rumor factory. The village of Sunan, in Korea, from which Jack London was ordered back to Seoul, is the farthest point north reached by an American or English correspondent. It is within a comparatively short distance of the Japanese firing line.

TRAGIC MAN HUNT IN THE STREETS OF SAN JOSE

'SMITES THE HAND THAT FED HIM'

Roosevelt's Attitude Toward Senator Burton, Who Helped to Make the White House Occupant the Vice-President.

BURTON'S FRIENDS ARE INDIGNANT

[Special by leased wire, the longest in the world.]
WASHINGTON, April 24.—President Roosevelt, Senator Long and Governor Bailey of Kansas have joined hands in a combination to unseat Senator Burton of Kansas, convicted and sentenced by the courts.

This powerful combination means to get in its work before Congress adjourns.

At present Governor Bailey is in Vermont, with Washington in view as his destination this week.

The immediate purpose of the combinationists is to create a vacancy in the Senate which Governor Bailey can fill by the appointment of Fourth Assistant Postmaster-General Bristow.

The story of this sensational development goes deep into the complications of Kansas politics and involves the recital of the likes and dislikes of the Roosevelt Administration. The complete history is a tale of political ingratitude.

FACTION LOSING ITS GRIP.

With recent months the faction known as the Long-Leland-Bailey faction has lost its firm grip upon Kansas politics. If the Senate postpones action upon Burton's case until the courts of appeal can be heard from, another election will roll around in which all the chances are against the success of the former political rulers. But if the Senate can be induced to cast out its Jonah at this session the vacancy will be filled by Governor Bailey. This is where the President enters the game. Knowing his partiality to Bristow, who has been at the bottom of the conviction of Burton and others, Senator Long appealed to him, with the promise that Bailey would appoint Bristow.

Still another factor entered strongly into the situation. Since he has been President, Mr. Roosevelt has given Senator Burton the marble heart. Although Burton was largely responsible for Roosevelt's nomination for vice-president at Philadelphia, when he went to Roosevelt and, acting for Senator Platt, prevailed upon Mr. Roosevelt to accept the vice-presidency nomination, the President forgot the hand that had elevated him. He spurned Burton's friendship long before Burton had lost his regular standing in the Republican party. Since the Burton conviction the presidential animosity against Burton has greatly increased and the sentiment at the White House is that he should be thrown out of the Senate by the back door.

DISLIKE TO BRISTOW.

A feature of the situation that may not have occurred to the President, who has become so accustomed to having his own way with Congress, is the fact that Bristow is the man whose latest report cast a deeply resented slur upon Senators of both parties. The Republican leaders, moreover, have made up their minds to leave Burton alone until the Appellate Court is heard from and they may not relish the idea of turning Burton out to put Bristow in. It is certain that it would be a bitter pill for many of them to take.

Burton's Republican friends are indig-

CLUBMAN HAS FIGHT WITH HIS POLITICIAN

Morgan's Saloon Scene of Early Morning Row That Promised a Tragedy.

Harry Gray, contractor, and Phil Crimmins, Republican boss, had a disgraceful fight in Morgan's saloon on Eddy street last Saturday morning about 2 o'clock.

Gray had several Bohemian Club friends with him. Crimmins had a coterie of followers, including "Peck" Eppinger.

Gray and Crimmins got into an altercation about Crimmins handling certain Supervisors in favor of Gray's rock-crushing operations. Both men had been up late and evidently had been very convivial in the various resorts they had gone to before winding up at the so-called "center-of-the-night" district.

Morgan offered the men books or auto-

as quickly as possible pulled him away and in vain tried to get him out of the saloon.

As soon as Gray gave him the indignity of a blow from his fist Crimmins rushed out of the Morgan saloon to get a gun. In the meantime Gray and his friends had another battle. While they were drinking it Crimmins returned with "Peck" Eppinger. Eppinger kicked Gray. Gray's friends succeeded in getting him in a hack.

JAPANESE SOLDIERS EATING AFTER A HARD MARCH, PHOTOGRAPHED EXCLUSIVELY FOR 'THE EXAMINER' BY JACK LONDON.

THE FACT THAT JACK LONDON HAS BEEN ABLE TO SEND EXCLUSIVE PHOTOGRAPHS OF THIS TYPE FROM THE SEAT OF WAR TO 'THE EXAMINER' IS ONE OF THE REASONS FOR THE ANTAGONISM OF THE OTHER CORRESPONDENTS, WHO HAVE FAILED TO GET BEYOND JAPAN.

1 KILLED; 22 HURT IN S. P. TRAIN WRECK

Unscheduled Engine Crashes Into a Train Carrying U. S. Soldiers Near Needles—Many of the Injured May Die.

[Special Dispatch to "The Examiner."]
NEEDLES (Cal.), April 24.—An engine going East unscheduled ran head on into a special loaded with United States troops five miles west of here this morning at about 11:30. An infantryman named Eugene Kuhn, from Duluth, Minn., was killed and twenty-two others injured, some of them seriously. Engineer Thompson of the light engine was badly bruised, but will recover.

EXPLOSIONS FOLLOW SHOWER OF METEORS

Unusual Occurrence Witnessed Off the Coast of Chile.

"EXAMINER" WRITER SENT BACK TO SEOUL

Men Sent By Other Papers Didn't Know How To Get to Firing Line.

BY JACK LONDON,
Special Commissioner of "The Examiner" to the Orient.

SEOUL, Korea, March 28.—A war is like a tea party—whoever gives it runs it, and the guests must smile and be polite, no matter how bored they may be. At present Japan is running the war, with Russia a lagging assistant, while the correspondents are trying to smile and be as polite as they can. They began to arrive in Japan early in January, and here, at the end of March, the majority of them are still in Japan. They are still in Japan because their kind hosts, the Japanese, have not yet given them permission to proceed to the front.

There are no signs that such permission will be given them anywhere in the near future, but they are an optimistic lot, these correspondents, and they still cherish the belief that they will arrive at the front in time for the finish. In the meantime they are wined and dined by their hosts and spend the rest of their time in receiving dispatches of the following nature from their papers: "Why no Tokio news?" "What is the matter with the Tokio service?" "Why no news from the front?"

Every little while—so I am given to understand—they get together and

ROBBER SHOT TO DEATH BY POLICE

Lone Highwayman Holds Up a San Jose Club and Desperate Man Hunt Follows Through the Streets of the Garden City

BULLETS FLY IN A RUNNING BATTLE

[Special Dispatch to "The Examiner."]
SAN JOSE, April 24.—A fierce battle to the death between a robber and the police was fought early this morning in the streets of San Jose. The robber was Bert Thorndyke, well known both here and in San Francisco; the crime, a hold-up at the Del Monte Club; the peace officers, Policemen Swanson, Geddis and Langford; the result, Thorndyke fatally shot by Policeman Swanson.

It had every element of a desperate man hunt. It was a frontier affray with a metropolitan setting and civilized characters. Even the villain, the hunted man, the desperado, was a man of position among his fellow men and at worst not a criminal by trade. In fact, it was his first offense. But despite the modern scenario there were still the primitive elements of a hold-up that might have occurred in some border town in the days when justice was dispensed over the limb of a tree or more often delivered in cold lead. There was the quick alarm; the rush of feet; the rattle of the fusillade; the hunt in the dark; the fugitive at bay; the last futile stand and the quick shot that brought with it the death moan and end.

HOW THE ROBBER WORKED.

Thorndyke's was not a spectacular crime. His victims thought at first it was a joke. Seven men were busy around the tables at the Del Monte, a private gambling club on South First street shortly before 1 o'clock, when Thorndyke quietly entered. He was masked and carried a revolver. His sharp demand for money brought every one in the room to attention, and with leveled weapon the robber advanced toward William George, the dealer. George passed over the bank roll of $375 with a laugh, for he believed some factious member was executing a hoax.

"Perhaps you'd like to have this ring, too," suggested George, smiling. He pointed to a large diamond that glittered on his hand.

"Yes, I'll take that too." There was grim directness in the bandit's answer, and he emphasized his command by pressing the muzzle of his revolver against George's side.

With alacrity the dealer slipped the jewel from his finger, the bandit took

↑
Spanish–American War: the
13th US Infantry Regiment
embarks for Cuba – Tampa,
Florida, 1898.

→
Colonel Theodore Roosevelt
posing in front of his Rough
Riders at the top of San
Juan Hill, which they had just
captured, Cuba, 1898.

Japanese representatives found themselves subject to American mediation. The Tsar had to cede Korea and the region of Port Arthur to Japan, along with part of the Sakhalin Islands between Russia and Japan. His troops were also forced to evacuate South Manchuria, which was returned to China.

For his role in resolving the conflict, President Theodore Roosevelt received the Nobel Peace Prize. He had just demonstrated to the world the ability of the United States to bring their full weight to bear on international geopolitics. For several years, America had undoubtedly wanted to extend its political and economic influence beyond its borders.

As early as 1898, the Spanish-American War permitted the US government to challenge Spain for control of its colonial possessions in the Caribbean and Pacific. The fighting, which took place mainly in Cuba, Puerto Rico and Manila, lasted barely three months and ended in an overwhelming victory for the United States. With the Treaty of Paris, Spain ceded the Philippines, Puerto Rico, and the island of Guam, in the Mariana Islands archipelago. The European country was also forced to recognize the independence of Cuba, which came under American control.

Lieutenant Theodore Roosevelt played a pivotal role at the Battle of San Juan Hill during the capture of Cuba and has been a national hero ever since. When he became president in 1902, America adopted the Big Stick policy: it positioned itself as a moral force, authorized to intervene militarily far and wide to defend its interests. This newly formed reality of American influence in the rest of the world often guided Jack London's footsteps in his travels to South America, Asia and throughout the Pacific.

↑
Postcard commemorating the Treaty of Portsmouth between Russia and Japan, achieved through American mediation. New York, Rotograph Company, 1905. Inset, from left to right: Tsar Nicholas II, President Theodore Roosevelt and Mikado Mutsu Hito.

THE VALLEY OF

THE MOON

On the ship from Japan back to the United States, Jack learned that Bessie had filed for divorce on the grounds of abandonment of the marital home and cruelty. When he arrived in San Francisco, the scandal had already spread to all the newspapers in the country.

His literary success, along with his nonconforming personality and fiery political convictions, had made him a media figure who fascinated the general public. His name, and often his face, was known to all. He was undoubtedly the first writer to trigger such a phenomenon, and journalists had made a habit of commenting on his every move and opinion.

Bessie requested that her husband's income and bank accounts be frozen for the duration of the proceedings. The process drew to a close on November 11, 1904: the divorce was decreed, and Bessie won the construction of a new house plus the custody of their daughters, Joan and Becky, then aged four and three years.

← ↑
Jack London in the Valley of the Moon.

↓
San Francisco Call article, July 1, 1904.

This judgment marked a turning point for Jack. He was 28 and a famous writer who had just published two stunningly successful books that received both public and critical acclaim: *The Call of the Wild* and *The Sea Wolf.* For months, he had remained discreet about his liaison with Charmian Kittredge. She was five years older than him, with a free and independent disposition and feminist ideas that were the opposite of Bessie's Victorian rigidity. Jack and Charmian fell madly in love in the summer of 1903. With Charmian, Jack had finally found his match—intelligent, ambitious and modern—with whom he could share everything, even his most daring projects.

They settled in the Sonoma Valley, about 45 miles north of San Francisco. It was farmland, but also wilderness, carpeted with oaks, firs and redwoods, where Jack would later declare that he had found his paradise, which he ardently described in *The Valley of the Moon* and *The Little Lady of the Big House.*

"I've a feeling as if we've just started to live"[1] (*The Valley of the Moon*).

Charmian Kittredge, the new Mrs. London.

Jack and Charmian at Wake Robin Lodge, in the Valley of the Moon, circa 1905.

↑
Charmian in the Valley of the Moon. An excellent rider, she was one of the first women in California to ride astride.

←
Jack in the Valley of the Moon in 1906. He loved horses and had learned to ride during his stay in Korea in 1904.

The Valley of the Moon

The Valley of the Moon (New York, The Macmillan Co., 1913) is a true declaration of Jack London's love of the property he had chosen to anchor his life, "across sheer ridges of the mountains, separated by deep green canyons and broadening lower down into rolling orchards and vineyards."[2]

At the beginning of the novel, the main characters (Billy, a young carter, and Saxon, a laundress) live in San Francisco, in a working-class world. Billy is imprisoned for having participated in a strike that had escalated. When he is released, the couple decides to move away from the city they feel has become too inhumane. Like Jack, they discover a simple and rural life in the Valley of the Moon and plan to build a ranch there.

When their dream begins to materialize, the arrival of a child seals their happiness.

↑
Jack at Wake Robin Lodge,
circa 1905.

In the village of Glen Ellen, Jack acquired a 130-acre property and hired a foreman to look after the crops. The couple moved to nearby Wake Robin Lodge, a summer residence owned by Charmian's aunt. The rhythm of the days was unchanging: every morning, Jack wrote his daily "thousand words," while Charmian used her stenographer and typist training to type the manuscripts on the Remington. The rest of the time was spent writing correspondence, horseback riding, swimming, relaxing and laughing by themselves or with the many friends they welcomed to their property.

In the Valley of the Moon, Jack embarked on his new Far North novel. On December 5, 1904, he wrote to George Brett, his publisher at The Macmillan Co.: "I have the idea for the next book I shall write . . . Not a Sequel to *Call of the Wild*. But a companion to *Call of the Wild*. I'm going to reverse the process. Instead of the devolution or decivilization of a dog, I'm going to give the evolution, the civilization of a dog."[3]

↑
Jack and Charmian swimming
at Wake Robin Lodge in the
summer of 1905.

↑
Jack, summer of 1905.

←
Charmian and Jack
practicing boxing. Jack
introduced his wife to his
favorite sport, Wake Robin
Lodge, circa 1905.

↑
Charmian, on the porch of Wake Robin Lodge, circa 1905.

←
Jack and Charmian in Jack's office at Wake Robin Lodge.

← Charmian photographed
by Jack in front of Morro
Castle, Havana, Cuba,
January 1906.

↗
The first view Jack and
Charmian had of Morro
Castle from their boat,
Havana, Cuba, January
1906 (photograph by
Jack London).

→
The wreck of *Maine* in
the port of Havana, Cuba,
1906 (photograph by
Jack London).

Charmian, on the porch of Wake Robin Lodge, circa 1905.

Jack and Charmian in Jack's office at Wake Robin Lodge.

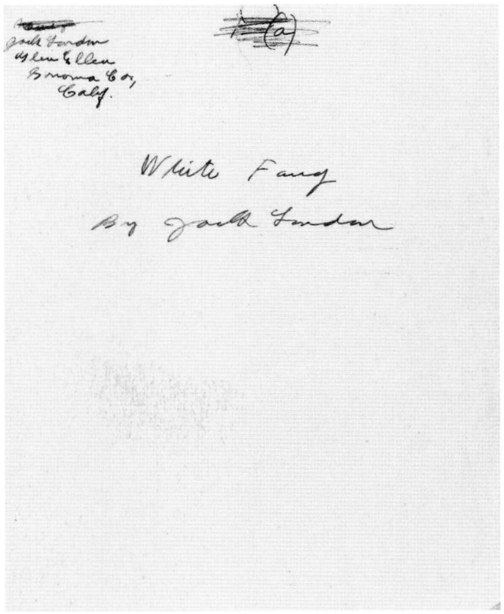

Jack London
Glen Ellen
Sonoma Co,
Calif.

White Fang

By Jack London

Part One

The Wild

Chapter I ---- The Trail of the Meat
Chapter II ---- The She-Wolf
Chapter III ---- The Hunger Cry

White Fang

Part One ---- The Wild
10,749
Chap. I --- The Trail of the Meat
" II ---- The She-Wolf.
" III ---- The Hunger-Cry.

Part Two ----- Born of the Wild
14,645
Chap. I ---- The Battle of the Fangs
" II ---- The Lair
" III ---- The Gray Cub.
" IV ---- The Wall of the World
" V ---- The Law of Meat.
25,394

Part Three ----- The Gods of the Wild.
Chapt. I ----- The Makers of Fire
" II ---- The Bondage.
" III ---- The Outcast.
" IV ---- The Trail of the Gods.
" V ---- The Covenant.
" VI ---- The Famine.

Part Four ----- The Superior Gods.
Chapter I ---- The Enemy of His Kind -
" II ---- The Mad God.
" III ---- The Reign of Hate.
" IV ---- The Clinging Death.
" V ---- The Indomitable.
" VI ---- The Love-Master.
(Over)

↑
White Fang manuscript: Title Page.

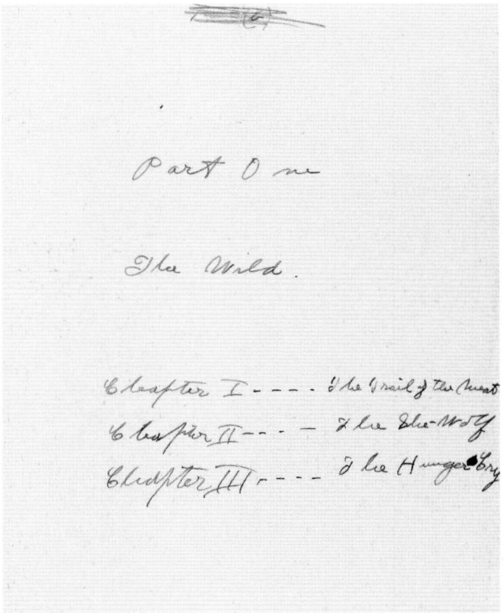

↗
White Fang manuscript: Summary.

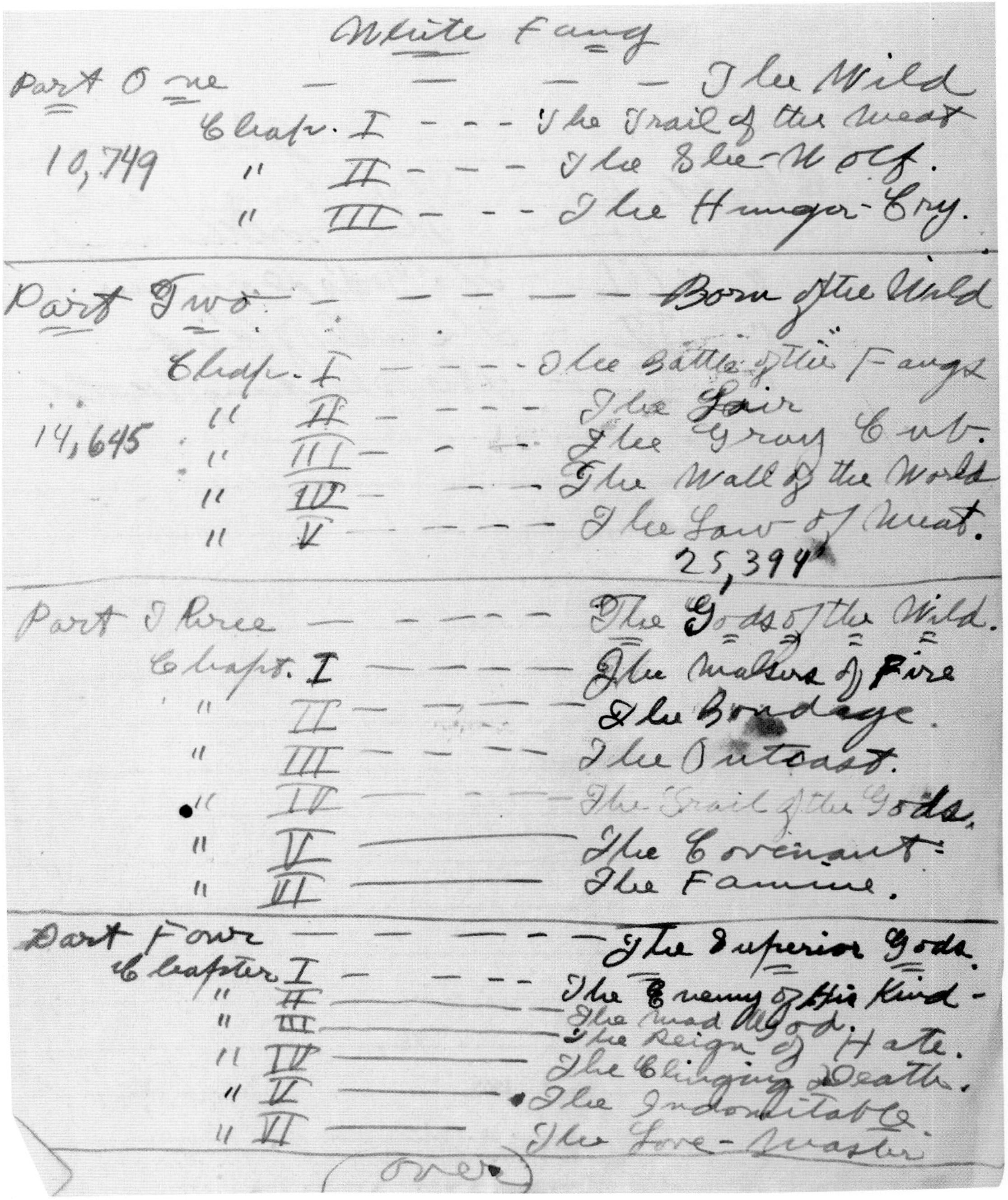

→
Cover of the original edition of *White Fang* (New York, The Macmillan Co., 1906).

→
Jack in his office at Wake Robin Lodge, where he wrote *White Fang*.

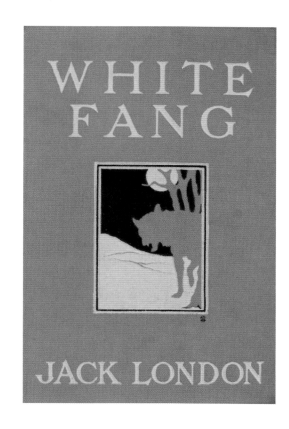

Published in October 1906, *White Fang* was an immediate success, especially among young readers. It was an indication of Jack's radical evolution, undoubtedly influenced by this happy stage of his life at Wake Robin, with Charmian at his side.

On November 18, 1905, after the mandatory one-year waiting period, the divorce with Bessie became final. The next day, Jack and Charmian got married in Chicago. For their honeymoon, they visited Jamaica, where they discovered the splendor of the Blue Mountains during rambles on horseback. Then they were off to Cuba, where they visited the major battle sites of the Spanish-American War, which had ended seven years earlier: San Juan Hill, where Theodore Roosevelt led his Rough Riders, Morro Castle and, of course, the wreck of the battleship Maine in the port of Havana. This trip would be the first in a long series, and for Jack, adventures would now be experienced with an enthusiastic partner. "We hated to leave Havana," Charmian wrote, "but all the world's before us!"[4]

Jack's literary success may have changed his life, but he retained his socialist ideals. In 1901, he left the Socialist Workers Party to join the newly founded Socialist Party of America and continued to declare his political views, at the risk of alienating readers and financial supporters. He published numerous virulent articles and pamphlets, notably in the official party journal, *The Comrade*, where he emphasized the need for a political struggle for American workers, and often closed his letters with: "Yours for the revolution."

←
Charmian photographed
by Jack in front of Morro
Castle, Havana, Cuba,
January 1906.

↗
The first view Jack and
Charmian had of Morro
Castle from their boat,
Havana, Cuba, January
1906 (photograph by
Jack London).

→
The wreck of *Maine* in
the port of Havana, Cuba,
1906 (photograph by
Jack London).

Prompted by the party's local division, who hoped to take advantage of his celebrity, Jack ran twice in the Oakland municipal elections in 1901 and 1905 as a Social Democrat candidate. In his campaign speeches, he openly attacked the American bourgeoisie vehemently: "You are drones that cluster around the capitalistic honey-vats ... Your fatuous self-sufficiency blinds you to the revolution that is surely, surely, coming, and which will as surely wipe you and your silk-lined, puffed-up leisure off the face of the map. You are parasites on the back of labor."[6] His viewpoints triggered blazing reactions in the press. The *San Francisco Newsletter* of March 25, 1905, stated: "London is no socialist. He is a firebrand and red-flag anarchist . . . and he should be arrested and prosecuted for treason."[7]

Jack was convinced that people had a pressing need to take their destiny in their hands as a group or they would otherwise be unable to overcome the oppression that held them victim. In 1905, he again triggered a scandal by publically taking sides with the Russian revolutionaries. Tsar Nicholas II's catastrophe against the Empire of Japan in Korea had weakened his authority, and workers and peasants had revolted. When troops opened fire on a crowd of protesters on January 22, 1905, in St. Petersburg, the country erupted. Strikes, occupations and attacks followed one after another. The culmination was reached in October, with a general strike that forced the tsar to soften— for a time—his position. Jack declared, "I speak, and I think, of the assassins in Russia as 'my comrades.' So do all the comrades in America."[8]

"Yours for the revolution."[5]

← Publication of Jack London's "Revolution" in *The International Socialist Review*, August 1909 (first published in *The Contemporary Review*, January 1908). Jack London denounces the blindness and greed of the "capitalist class," and calls for revolution.

Jack also had a close relationship with another famous activist in the Socialist Party of America: Upton Sinclair, author of the novel *The Jungle*, which denounces the terrible living and working conditions of slaughterhouse workers in Chicago. The book launched a broadside against President Roosevelt that would compel him to appoint an investigative committee. Jack fiercely defended Sinclair in the press: "What *Uncle Tom's Cabin* did for black slaves, *The Jungle* has a large chance to do for the white slaves of today . . . It is written of sweat and blood, and groans and tears. It depicts, not what man ought to be, but what man is compelled to be in this, our world, in the twentieth century. It will open countless ears that have been deaf to socialism."[10]

In 1905, Sinclair founded the Intercollegiate Socialist Society (ISS). The organization was intended to attract students from major universities to the socialist ranks, where the future elite of the nation would be formed. Jack was elected president and, between 1905 and 1906, conducted a series of 30 lectures across the country. He delivered political speeches at Harvard and Yale to an audience of more than 3,000 people, including professors, students, workers, activists and journalists.

While Jack London's political commitment was often misunderstood in the United States, it made him incredibly popular in Russia. More than 30 million of his books would be sold, and even Lenin, on his deathbed, asked his wife to reread him one of Jack's Klondike stories!

"Nothing will withstand us, for the strength of each man will be the strength of all men in the world."[9]

In his futuristic novel *The Iron Heel* (New York, The Macmillan Co., 1906), Jack London imagines a socialist government voted into power in the United States, their failure and the process that then allows the capitalist opposition to ultimately crush the working class, with its "iron heel," by establishing a dictatorship.

"The Dream of Debs"

In January and February 1909, the *International Socialist Review* published "The Dream of Debs" by Jack London. Jack chose Eugene Debs, one of the leading figures of the Socialist Party of America, as his main character for the short story. He founded one of the first American industrial unions, the American Railway Union, in 1893 and was sentenced to six months in prison the following year for participating in the Chicago strikes. While in detention, he discovered Marx's work, and after his release started a career as a politician by joining the Socialist Party. He stood as candidate in the presidential elections five times, in 1900, 1904, 1908, 1912 and 1920.

In "The Dream of Debs," London imagines, not without irony, how a general strike manages to paralyze San Francisco and plunge the bourgeois of the city into famine, forcing them to yield to demands. Eugene Debs was also Jack's inspiration for another short story: in the sci-fi tale "Goliath" (first published in *The Bookman* in February 1910), Percival Stutlz, a double of Debs, lives on an imaginary island off San Francisco. He has developed a secret weapon capable of annihilating any remote matter that he uses to threaten the governments of the great Western powers. After demonstrating its strength, he manages to bend them to his will and bring socialism to the world.

← Upton Sinclair.

The International Socialist Review

TEN CENTS
A COPY

ONE DOLLAR
A YEAR

Jack London
AUTHOR AND SOCIALIST

JANUARY 1909

JACK LONDON'S
LATEST STORY
The Dream of Debs
STARTS IN THIS ISSUE

RHChaplin '08

AND THE EARTH

SHOOK...

↓
Pages from *Around the World in the Sloop Spray* by Joshua Slocum (New York, Charles Scribner's Sounds, 1903): Joshua Slocum (left), *Spray* in a storm off New York (right). Jack baptized one of his first sailboats *Spray* in honor of the boat that took Captain Slocum on the first solo trip around the world, between 1895 and 1898. Reading Slocum's book also inspired *The Cruise of the Snark*.

←
San Francisco in flames following the earthquake, April 1906.

↑
The *Great White Fleet* in San Francisco, 1908.

Jack had no sooner arrived back in the Valley of the Moon when the tireless traveler began to dream of a new challenge for him and Charmian. Inspired by the story of Captain Joshua Slocum's solo world tour, he decided to build a sailboat and undertake a seven-year journey around the world. Baptized *Snark* in tribute to the Lewis Carroll tale, the boat would cross the Pacific Ocean, the China Sea and the Mediterranean Sea. She would sail through the Suez Canal and follow the great rivers, like the Yang Tse Kiang, the Nile and the Danube, to visit the capital cities located on the waterways. The Rhone and the Seine took him to Paris, where he anchored at the foot of Notre-Dame.

The analogy with President Roosevelt's grand plan at the time, an actual world tour of the American fleet, was striking. Unbridled American competition in an increasingly global market economy was driving an increase in naval forces. The United States had recently produced new, state-of-the-art steel battleships and had set up bases on foreign soil to welcome them, especially in the Pacific.

CAPTAIN SLOCUM.

The *Spray* in Storm off New York.

With stark white hulls leaving a strong impression, the 16 ships of the American Great White Fleet crisscrossed the oceans between 1907 and 1909. They traveled 43,000 nautical miles, making 20 port calls for friendly courtesy visits all over the globe. Above all, they displayed a tremendous show of strength to European colonial powers and Japan.

 Designed to accommodate a crew of six—in addition to Jack and Charmian—the *Snark* was a two-masted vessel estimated to cost $7,000. Equipped with a 70-horse auxiliary engine, she was

↖
Roscoe Eames (Charmian London's uncle and the *Snark*'s first captain), Charmian and Jack London, San Francisco, 1906.

↑
Jack photographs the *Snark* shipyard, 1906.

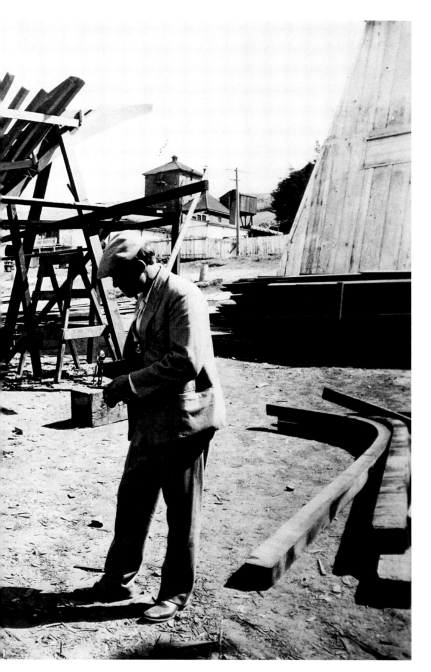

balanced on a 5-ton iron keel, and her hull was about 46 feet long. She was also equipped with large water tanks and could carry enough supplies for six months at sea.

Their departure was scheduled for October 1, 1906. Jack had a contract with the Anderson Ways shipyard of San Francisco, where the parts were assembled. But, just when the keel was about to be attached, work stopped abruptly, on April 18, 1906. Shortly after five o'clock in the morning, the earth shook in San Francisco.

↑
Jack and Charmian sitting on a partially constructed *Snark*, 1906.

←
Jack in the *Snark* shipyard,
1906.

↗
The construction of the *Snark*
at Anderson Ways shipyard,
San Francisco, 1906.

→
The *Snark* shipyard, 1906.

The disaster was unprecedented. San Francisco, with its many wooden buildings, was devoured by flames. For three days, firefighters and the public fought against the fire that ravaged everything in its path. In the end, 80 percent of the city was destroyed: three thousand dead and nearly 300,000 homeless.

Jack and Charmian also felt the tremors in the Sonoma Valley, where from a hill, they saw huge columns of smoke rising from the Bay. They immediately drove to San Francisco where they wandered for hours, overwhelmed by the spectacle before them.

"Here and there through the smoke, creeping warily under the shadows of tottering walls, emerged occasional men and women. It was like the meeting of the handful of survivors after the day of the end of the world."[1]

The Grand Hotel, Santa Rosa, California, destroyed by the earthquake, April 1906 (photograph by Jack London).

↑ ↗
San Francisco City Hall, April 1906 (photographs by Jack London). Description made by Jack in his article "The Story of an Eye-Witness," *Collier's*, May 5, 1906: "I was creeping past the shattered dome of the City Hall. Than it there was no better exhibit of the destructive force of the earthquake. Most of the stone had been shaken from the great dome, leaving standing the naked framework of steel."

Next double page: The Barbary Coast, San Francisco, April 1906 (photograph by Jack London).

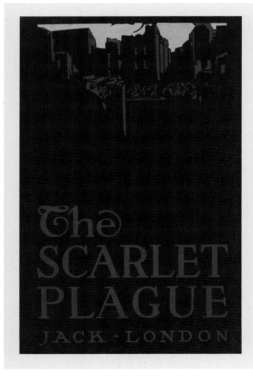

The Scarlet Plague

The apocalyptic vision of San Francisco destroyed by the earthquake largely inspired Jack London's *The Scarlet Plague* (Paris, Phoebus, 2006, New York, The Macmillan Co., 1915). In the novel, an old man and his grandson roam over a devastated land, which was once prosperous California. An unknown disease, the "scarlet plague," has killed almost all the inhabitants, and the cities are now in ruins.

↑
Smoking ruins in San Francisco devastated by the earthquake, April 1906 (photograph by Jack London).

↗
A few weeks after the earthquake, Jack (behind the wheel) and Charmian (in the back) return to San Francisco.

→
Cover of *Collier's* magazine, May 5, 1906, featuring Jack London's article, "The Story of an Eye-Witness."

Jack recorded details of the devastated city with his ubiquitous camera. Two weeks later, his emotions were still palpable when he told the story of the disaster in *Collier's* magazine: "Not in history has a modern imperial city been so completely destroyed. San Francisco is gone. Nothing remains of it but memories and a fringe of dwelling-houses on its outskirts. Its industrial section is wiped out. Its business section is wiped out. Its social and residential section is wiped out. The factories and warehouses, the great stores and newspaper buildings, the hotels and the palaces of the nabobs, are all gone."[2]

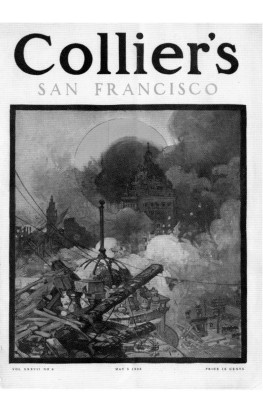

The magnitude of recent events completely upset the Londons' fixed schedule for their cruise around the world. Reconstructing the city was a priority, and the *Snark* shipyard directly suffered the consequences. Deliveries were delayed, when they were not purely and simply canceled. The initial cost was multiplied by five because wages and the prices of material exploded. A victim of dishonest suppliers, Jack also discovered multiple defects, and a first round of sea trials revealed fatal design errors. Jack was increasingly the target of cutting comments from journalists. Exasperated, he decided to leave and go to Hawaii to finish the work. On April 23, 1907, nearly a year late, the *Snark* finally left Oakland and set off into the Pacific under the eyes of thousands of onlookers gathered to witness the highly anticipated launch.

↖
The *Snark*'s first test run. Jack is at the helm, Charmian on his left, 1907.

↑
Roscoe Eames, captain of the *Snark*, 1907.

↗
Jack London on the *Snark* bridge the day she was launched, Oakland, 1907.

→
Jack sitting on *Snark*'s bowsprit during tests, 1907.

Next double page: The *Snark* at the quay the day of her launch, Oakland, 1907.

1907 — 1908

ACROSS THE

PACIFIC

From the very beginning of the trip, Jack realized that his crew was drastically inexperienced. He was, actually, the only one to have ever sailed beyond San Francisco Bay. In fact, Captain Roscoe Eames—Charmian's uncle—turned out to be completely incompetent, and Jack had to quickly learn the basics of deep-sea sailing in order to keep *Snark* heading in the right direction. The general atmosphere deteriorated and discipline disintegrated as everyone suffered from seasickness.

In addition, the boat responded poorly and often refused to sail close to the wind. Damages proliferated. At the first storm, the ship took on water from all sides, demolishing the engine room. The fuel tank leaked and flooded the food supply compartment; the engine, commissioned at a premium price from New Jersey, was unusable, and had to be dragged out on deck; when the spinnaker was hoisted, the boom gave way, and the sail had to be hauled down.

←
The *Snark*'s stern, between 1907 and 1908.

↑
Captain Roscoe Eames (left) during the crossing from San Francisco to Hawaii, 1907.

However, this first experience on the high seas aboard the *Snark* enchanted Jack and Charmian. Their dream was taking shape, and they marveled at the sight of the stars, whales and flying fish. After four weeks of sailing, they spied the summits of Mauna Kea and Haleakala, the largest extinct volcano in the world. They crossed the reefs bordering Oahu Island and anchored in Honolulu Harbor on May 20, 1907.

During this first leg of the voyage, the Londons were still on American soil. The Republic of Hawaii had been annexed ten years previously, which allowed the United States to occupy a strategic position in this region of the world. The base at Pearl Harbor had been designed to accommodate large steamships for refueling with coal on the route to other Pacific Islands and Asia.

The modifications the *Snark* needed, as well as the engine repairs, imposed a long stopover. Jack sent the crew back to California thinking he would recruit a new one. The only exception was Martin Johnson, the young cook, whom he promoted to mechanic. And while the work was being done at a shipyard in Honolulu, he and Charmian decided to set off to discover the other islands of the archipelago.

"Abruptly the land itself, in a riot of olive-greens of a thousand hues, reached out its arms and folded the *Snark* in."[1]

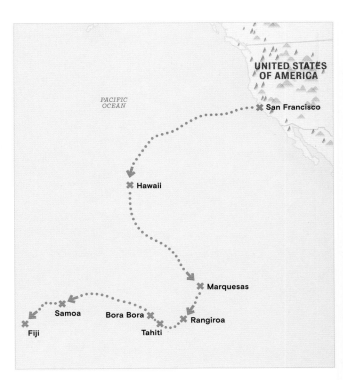

Jack London on the *Snark*
bridge in 1907, taking their
position with a sextant: "I was
not as other men—most other
men; I knew what they did
not know,—the mystery of the
heavens, that pointed out the
way across the deep."[2]

→

Jack and Charmian London
aboard the *Snark* between
1907 and 1908.

↑
In Hawaii, Jack London
(center right) is fascinated
by outrigger canoes, Waikiki
Beach, Oahu, 1907.

→
The *Snark* moored in Pearl
Harbor, Hawaii, 1907.

At first, the Londons shared the life and pastimes of the American community on Oahu; they swam at Waikiki, attended polo matches and various parties along with the governor and other notables. Then, at the request of the president of the Board of Health, they spent a week on the island of Molokai, a dreadful place housing a large colony of lepers. Preparing to write the article, Jack, as usual, thoroughly documented his subject. He took numerous photographs on Molokai and spent long periods talking with the medical staff. The couple was then off to the islands of Maui and Hawaii, where they were welcomed on ranches and coffee and sugar cane plantations. Jack and Charmian also headed out on horseback or on foot to ramble amid spectacular mountain panoramas, home to volcanoes, jungles and waterfalls.

Back in Hilo, they found the *Snark* and her new captain, James Warren Langhorne, a former convict to whom Jack had decided to give a second chance. The crew also included three other newcomers: Hermann De Visser, a Dutch sailor; Wada, a Japanese cook; and Nakata, a young Hawaiian ship boy.

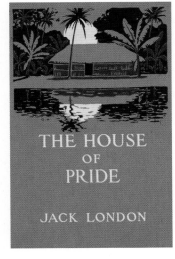

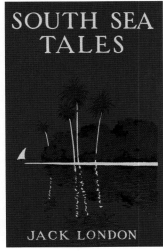

←
Original covers of *The House of Pride* (New York, The Macmillan Co., 1912) and *South Sea Tales* (New York, The Macmillan Co., 1911). The short stories in these collections are a testament to London's admiration for the people of the Hawaiian archipelago, their values and their culture.

Charmian London exploring
the shores of Molokai Island on
horseback, Hawaii, 1907.

→
Rainbow Falls, Hilo, Hawaii,
1907 (photograph by Jack
London).

After five months spent in the archipelago, on October 7, 1908, the *Snark* sailed off for the next major leg of its journey: the Marquesas and French Polynesia. This new crossing, which lasted sixty days, was filled with adventures. The engines broke down, and they could only move under sail to find favorable winds that would blow them toward the Marquesas in the southeast, while the currents pulled them toward the south and threatened to prolong the voyage dangerously. The situation was further complicated when a faucet inadvertently left open severely depleted their supply of drinking water and forced them to ration. To save water, no one washed, and Jack let his beard and mustache grow.

"Our memories of the world, the great world, became like dreams of former lives we had lived somewhere before we came to be born on the *Snark*."[3]

Fortunately, Captain Warren Langhorne was an excellent sailor and handled the *Snark* with authority. Jack felt confident, and all enjoyed the days that flowed by, punctuated by various activities. Fishing, of course, in these waters where fish teemed: skipjack, kakous—kinds of sea pike—turtles, a dolphin, and even a shark 10 feet long that had to be hoisted on board to be chopped up. Physical exercises, too: push-ups, hanging from the rail of the hatch ladder or boxing matches between Jack and Charmian, who did not forget to pack their gloves. In the afternoon, Jack reread frequently aloud to his companions, the works of Melville and

↖
Jack London (left) pulls in his catch on the *Snark*, between 1907 and 1908.

↖
Shark hauled aboard the *Snark* between 1907 and 1908: "Sharks we caught occasionally, on large hooks, with chain-swivels, bent on a length of small rope."[4]

↑
Martin Johnson displays the jaw of a shark caught from the *Snark* to Jack London's lens, between 1907 and 1908.

Next double page: The *Snark*'s bow, between 1907 and 1908.

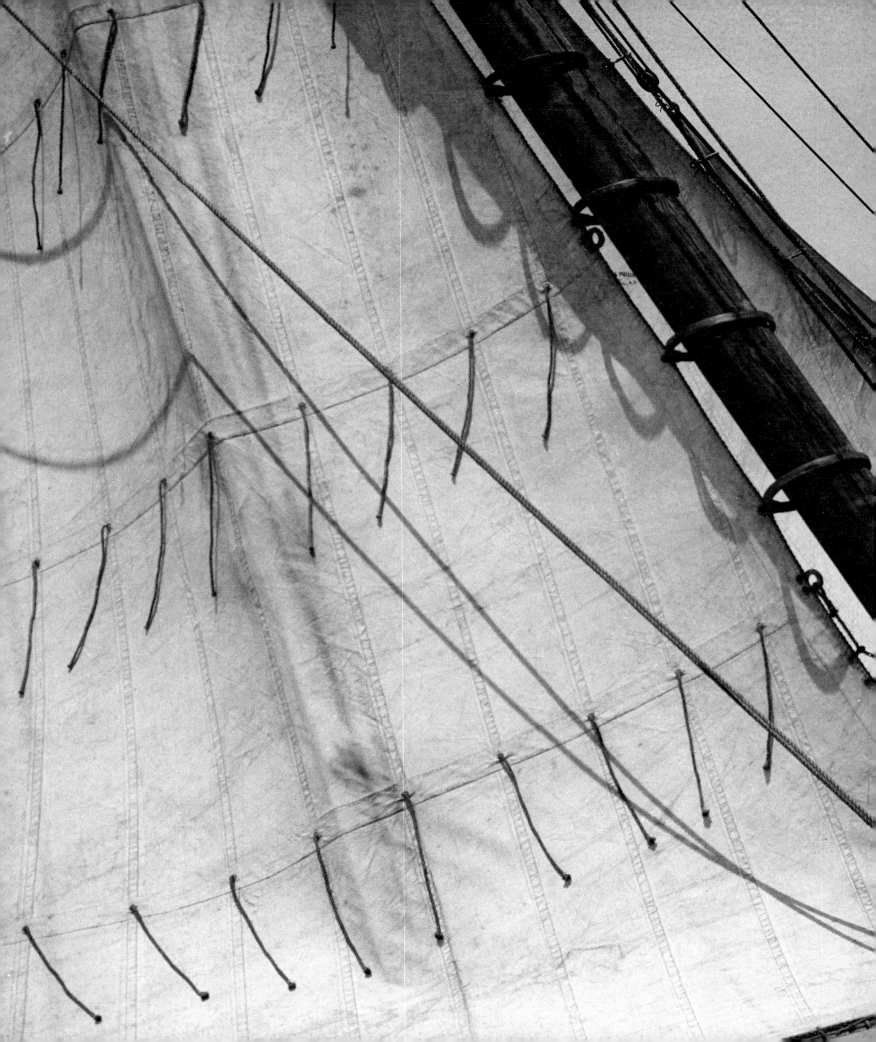

← The *Snark* moored at Hilo in the Hawaiian Islands, 1907.

↗ First page of manuscript of Chapter IX "A Pacific Traverse," *The Cruise of the Snark* (New York, The Macmillan Co., 1911).

→ Last page of manuscript of Chapter VII "The Lepers Of Molokai," *The Cruise of the Snark* (New York, The Macmillan Co., 1911). At the bottom of the page, Jack London specified the place where the chapter was written, "Waikiki, Oahu, in July 11, 1907."

Stevenson recounting their journeys in this region of the world a few years earlier. Long card games enlivened the evenings. And Jack and Charmian spent their nights lying on folded canvases on the deck, to better observe the moon.

They lived in a bubble unaffected by time, as Jack would later attest: "There were no guests to dinner, no telegrams, no insistent telephone jangles invading our privacy. We had no engagements to keep, no trains to catch, and there were no morning newspapers over which to waste time in learning what was happening to our fifteen hundred million other fellow-creatures."[5]

Much of the day was, as always, devoted to writing. Hermann and Captain Warren Langhorne set up a tent above the cockpit to allow Charmian and Jack to work out of the sun. She kept the ship's log, while he launched into a new strongly autobiographical novel, *Martin Eden*.

Often considered Jack London's masterpiece today, the main character of the book is a young sailor who wants to become a writer and recounts his superhuman efforts to achieve his goal. Martin Eden works tirelessly to develop a new and sincere personal style, drawing his truth from his own experiences. "His work was realism, though he endeavored to fuse it with the fancies and beauties of imagination," explained Jack. "What he sought was an impassioned realism, shot through with human aspiration and faith. What he wanted was life as it was, with all its spirit-groping and soul-reaching left in."[6] But, while literary success brings Martin Eden fortune and fame, it removes all his illusions, leaving him no other option but suicide. Having decided to flee the Californian conformist society whose prejudices disgust him, he jumps from the steamship taking him to Hawaii and is carried away by the sea.

On November 19, Jack and Charmian celebrated their two years of marriage on board and broke open a bottle of cider for the occasion. A week later, the *Snark* finally managed to catch a wind that pushed it southeast, all the way to the Marquesas Islands. After being lashed by several squalls, they reached Nuku Hiva Island on December 6, 1907, and anchored in Taiohae Bay.

Nuku Hiva was the only island in the Marquesan archipelago that the *Snark* visited. They stayed there for two weeks. For Jack and Charmian, this stopover was highly symbolic, because the valley of Typee, long described by Herman Melville in the novel that

"We were heaven-directed, and it was I who could read the sign-post of the sky!—I! I!"[7]

↑
Marquesan islanders posing next to the Londons' gramophone, Nuku Hiva Island, Marquesas, December 1907 (photograph by Jack London).

↗
Prepublication of Chapter X of *The Cruise of the Snark*, named by Jack London after the Herman Melville novel: Typee, Pacific Monthly, March 1910.

→
Jack London in the Pacific Islands, between 1907 and 1908.

bears this title, was located here. Sadly, where Melville described a lively farming valley, populated by 2,000 vigorous inhabitants, there were only ruins overrun by the primeval forest where a few dozens of miserable natives, ravaged by leprosy, elephantiasis and tuberculosis, lived.

The island, however, offered them some exceptional moments: they rode through the forest on Marquesan ponies, hunted wild goats in the Hakaui valley and discovered a little paradise in the Hooumi valley containing banana, coconut and breadfruit trees and emerald waterfalls. On several occasions, they organized gramophone sessions, where they introduced Caruso, Schubert and popular American tunes to the fascinated indigenous population.

They purchased many traditional items and clothing—sarongs, belted dance skirts, carved calabashes, Tuamotu pearls, carved paddles and models of war canoes. They entrusted their carefully packaged souvenirs to an outbound schooner. During the cruise of the *Snark*, dozens of items were collected and shipped to the Londons' home in California.

Once stocked with fresh mangoes, lemons, coconuts, chickens, fish, fresh water and even bread, found in a French bakery (!), the *Snark* set sail on the night of December 18, 1907, with only the moon to light her way. They set sail for Tahiti, where lagoons and coral reefs awaited.

Charmian and Jack celebrated Christmas 1907 on the open sea, while the *Snark* faced a perfect storm. After nine days of an exceptionally strenuous crossing, they finally drew in sight of Tahiti and moored at Papeete on December 26.

To their great amazement, they discovered that, with no news of them since their departure from Hawaii, they had been believed

LOOKING BACK FROM THE DIVIDE BETWEEN TYPEE AND HO-O-U-MI.

Typee

By Jack London

Author of "Call of the Wild," "Martin Eden," "Sea Wolf," etc.

TO the eastward Ua-huka was being blotted out by an evening rain-squall that was fast overtaking the *Snark*. But that little craft, her big spinnaker filled by the southeast trade, was making a good race of it. Cape Martin, the southeast-ermost point of Nuku-hiva, was abeam, and Comptroller Bay was opening up as we fled past its wide entrance, where Sail Rock, for all the world like the spritsail of a Columbia River salmon-boat, was making brave weather of it in the smashing southeast swell.

"What do you make that out to be?" I asked Herman, at the wheel.

"A fishing-boat, sir," he answered, after careful scrutiny.

Yet on the chart it was plainly marked, "Sail Rock."

But we were more interested in the recesses of Comptroller Bay, where our eyes eagerly sought out the three bights of land and centered on the midmost one, where the gathering twilight showed the dim walls of a valley extending inland. How often we had pored over the chart and centered always on that midmost bight and on the valley it opened—the Valley of Typee. "Taipi," the chart

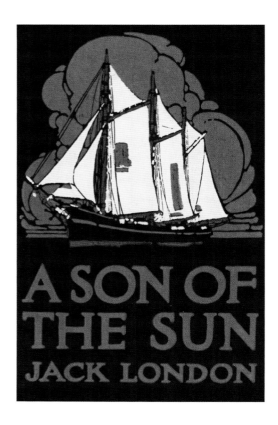

The *Snark* in Taiohae Bay,
Nuku Hiva, Marquesas Islands,
December 1907.

Original cover of *A Son of the
Sun* (New York, Doubleday,
1912). In one of the short
stories, "The Pearls of Parlay,"
Jack denounces the racism of
the Papeete citizens and the
greed of the pearl traffickers.

to be lost at sea. And the mail, which had been waiting for them in Tahiti for weeks, revealed a catastrophic situation back in California: due to Charmian's aunt's gross mismanagement, their affairs in California were in turmoil. The *Snark* once again required repairs—the engine had to be removed again—so they decided to make a quick trip to California on an ocean liner while the work was being done, to put their finances in order and restore the confidence of the banks. A month later, their financial situation recovered, and they were back in Polynesia.

Despite its splendor, Tahiti disappointed them. Papeete is a bit like the "Paris of the Pacific," and, as Charmian noted in the ship's log, the country, "although surpassingly beautiful … is very much on the 'tourist route.'"[9]

After a short stop in Moorea, they set sail on April 4, 1908, for Raiatea. There, Jack and Charmian made a pivotal encounter: a fisherman, Tehei, came to meet them on an outrigger canoe with a broad sail and invited them to board his boat to sail to his home, on the island of Taha'a, located about six miles away. "I found my breath coming quickly at the proximity of some of the large coral masses," Charmian remembers, "but Tehei perched in the stern and serenely steered with a big paddle overside, winding in and out the little channels of the reef, familiar to him as our city streets to us."[10]

"It is good to ride the tempest and feel godlike."[8]

←
James Warren Langhorne, captain of the *Snark*, Papeete, Tahiti, 1908.

→
Tahiti, 1908 (photograph by Jack London).

For two days, Tehei and his royal wife, Bihouara, offered the Londons island hospitality. They welcomed the couple to their hut, where they were honored with a veritable feast before being shown around the village; Tehei introduced them to traditional fishing methods in his dugout canoe. When the *Snark* resumed her journey, the bridge was covered with bananas, coconuts and papayas brought by the inhabitants of the island; chickens ran in all directions, and even a suckling pig struggled like a demon! Tehei and Bihouara were also on board, invited by Jack and Charmian to accompany them to Bora Bora. Their presence certainly played a role in the exceptional hospitality the Londons received there. Before a dream-like backdrop, a percussion concert punctuated the dances of the vahines and their male partners, who donned their finest adornments. A

"Perhaps the most delightful feature of [their hospitality] was that it was due to no training, to no complex social ideals, but that it was the untutored and spontaneous outpouring from their hearts."[11]

gigantic fishing party was even organized in their honor. A hundred boatmen whipped the water with stones attached to the end of ropes, to drive the fish toward shore.

And when the *Snark* set off for far-off Samoa, she carried a new crewmember: Tehei, temporarily leaving his wife in Bora Bora, decided to join the Londons on their journey.

On the route to Samoa, Tehei, an excellent sailor, proved to be invaluable and sometimes even took the helm. The weather was perfect and the temperatures balmy. In the cool of the evening, a cheerful mood reigned on board, nourished by the diversity of the crew: Tehei, Wada and Nakata demonstrated their country's dances, while Charmian sang, accompanying herself on the ukulele.

After 13 days at sea, the *Snark* was again in US territory. In 1899, nine years earlier, Germany and the United States had split up the archipelago of Samoa, the latter inheriting the eastern part. The Londons first went to the island of Tau, where the old

Traditional fishing organized in honor of the Londons, which became the subject of Chapter XIII of *The Cruise of the Snark*: "The Stone Fishing of Bora Bora." "He merely smites the water with the stone, pulls up the stone, and smites again. He goes on smiting. In the stern of each canoe another man paddles, driving the canoe ahead and at the same time keeping it in the formation"[12] (photograph by Jack London).

Jack and Charmian London, invited aboard Tehei's outrigger canoe, go to Taha'a Island, French Polynesia, April 1908.

Inhabitants of Bora Bora welcome the crew of the *Snark*, April 1908 (photograph by Jack London).

"THE NATURE MAN"

BY

JACK LONDON

FROM THE ISLAND OF TAHITI, IN THE
SOUTHERN SEAS, COMES ANOTHER OF
MR. LONDON'S FIRST-HAND ACCOUNTS
OF STRANGE PEOPLE IN STRANGE LANDS
WRITTEN FOR COMPANION READERS

The *Snark* at Anchor Off the Coast of Tahiti, Where Mr. London and His Wife and Crew Were Reported Lost. Mr. London is Playing Host; the Nature Man, Dressed in Full Calling Costume, is Sunning Himself on the Gunwale of the Boat

I FIRST met him on Market Street in San Francisco. It was a wet and drizzly afternoon, and he was striding along, clad solely in a pair of abbreviated knee trousers and an abbreviated shirt, his bare feet going slick-slick through the pavement slush. At his heels trooped a score of excited gamins. Every head —and there were thousands—turned to glance curiously at him as he went by. And I turned, too. Never had I seen such lovely sunburn. He was all sunburn, of the sort a blond takes on when his skin does not peel. His long yellow hair was burnt; so was his beard, which sprang from a soil unplowed by any razor. He was a tawny man, a golden-tawny man, all glowing and radiant with the sun. Another prophet, thought I, come up to town with a message that will save the world.

A few weeks later I was with some friends in their bungalow in the Piedmont Hills overlooking San Francisco Bay. "We've got him, we've got him," they barked. "We caught him up a tree; but he's all right now, he'll feed from the hand. Come on and see him." So I accompanied them up a dizzy hill, and in a rickety shack in the midst of a eucalyptus grove I found my sunburned

After a week or so my conscience smote me, and I invited him to dinner at a down-town hotel. He arrived, looking unwontedly stiff and uncomfortable in a cotton jacket. When invited to peel it off, he beamed his gratitude and joy, and did so, revealing his sun-gold skin, from waist to shoulder, covered only by a piece of fish net of coarse twine and large of mesh. A scarlet loin cloth completed his costume. I began my acquaintance with him that night, and during my long stay in Tahiti that acquaintance ripened into friendship.

"So you write books," he said one day, when, tired and sweaty, I finished my morning's work.

"I, too, write books," he announced.

Aha, thought I, now at last is he going to pester me with his literary efforts. My soul was in revolt. I had not come all the way to the South Seas to be a literary bureau.

"This is the book I write," he explained, smashing himself a resounding blow on the chest with his clenched fist. "The gorilla in the African jungle pounds his chest till the noise of it can be heard half a mile away."

"A pretty good chest," quoth I admiringly; "it would make even a gorilla envious."

And then, and later, I learned the details of the marvelous book Ernest Darling had written. Twelve years ago he lay close to death. He weighed but ninety pounds and was too weak to speak. The doctors had given him up. His father, a practising physician, had given him up. Consultations with other physicians had been held upon him. There was no hope for him. Overstudy (as a schoolteacher and as a university student) and two successive attacks of pneumonia were responsible for his breakdown. Day by day he was losing strength. He could extract no nutrition from the heavy foods they gave him; nor could pellets and powders help his stomach to do the work of digestion. Not only was he a physical wreck, but he was a mental wreck. His mind was overwrought. He was sick and tired of medicine, and he was sick and tired of persons. Human speech

↑
Prepublication of Chapter XI
of *The Cruise of the Snark*:
"The Nature Man," *Woman's
Home Companion*, September
1908. Jack London recounts
his meeting with Ernest Darling,
an eccentric American socialist
who chose to live in a hut,
close to nature, in the hills of
Papeete, Tahiti.

→
Last page of *The Cruise of
the Snark* manuscript: "The
High Seat of Abundance." At
the bottom of the page, Jack
London has indicated where
the chapter was written: "At
Sea, Between Bora Bora and
Samoa, April 24, 1908."

58

came back. Sometimes
they did not come
back. And in the con-
fusion, unobserved,
the little sucking-pig
got loose and slipped
overboard.

"On the arrival of
strangers, every man
endeavored to obtain
one as a friend and
carry him off to his own
habitation, where he is
treated with the greatest
kindness by the inhabit-
ants of the district; they
place him on a high
seat and feed him
with abundance of the
finest food."

Jack London

at Sea, Between Bora Bora
& Samoa, Apr. 24, 1908.

↑
Samoan village, May 1908
(photograph by Jack
London).

→
Samoan resident, May
1908 (photograph by Jack
London).

monarch Tuimanua organized lavish ceremonies for them. They then headed to Pago Pago, on the island of Tutuila, where there was an important Navy base, and were received this time by the governor and the American officers. In Apia, on Upolu Island, they stopped in the heart of a lush jungle to visit the grave of Robert Stevenson, well-known author of *Treasure Island*: "I wouldn't have gone out of my way to visit the grave of any other man in the world,"[13] Jack stated solemnly. And then, as they skirted the shores of the island of Savaï, they were witness to a horrific volcanic explosion. The lava flowed into the sea, destroying many villages; Charmian and Jack worked with the relief team for several days in the sweltering heat.

After a four-week stay in the Samoan archipelago, the *Snark* had traveled most of the initially planned route through the Pacific Islands: nearly 7,500 miles, during which they dropped anchor in areas where foreign domination, be it American or French, was striking. This adventure involved its share of risks but took place in dream-like settings alongside welcoming and often ethnically diverse populations. When they sailed on May 20, 1908, it was a very different journey to the one they started on. They set sail for the black islands of Melanesia, reputed to be hostile and inhospitable: Fiji, the New Hebrides and the Solomon Islands.

Jack London poses with two Samoan residents, May 1908.

← Charmian London in the Samoan archipelago, May 1908.

← The *Snark* in the Samoan archipelago, May 1908.

→ Jack London at the grave of writer Robert Louis Stevenson, Apia, Samoa, May 1908. The author of *Dr. Jekyll and Mr. Hyde* and *Treasure Island*, whom Jack London admired deeply, lived for four years in Samoa, where he was nicknamed Tusitala (storyteller).

At his death, on December 3, 1894, four hundred Samoan warriors carried his coffin to his grave.

He had written the epitaph himself, which begins with these words: "Under the wide and starry sky, dig the grave and let me lie. Glad did I live and gladly die."

THE BLACK

ISLANDS

"I know Adventure is not dead because I have had a long and intimate correspondence with Adventure."[1]

The weather also exhibited profound changes. Winter was advancing, the temperature was falling, and during the crossing to Fiji, the *Snark* had to battle violent squalls.

On board, the atmosphere was deteriorating: Captain Warren, now nicknamed "The Blight" by the rest of the crew, had become unbearable. His authoritarian fits were frequent and revealed an angry and aggressive temperament. He took a dislike to Wada, the Japanese cook, and harassed him to the point of breaking his nose. Isolated from the others, who distrusted him, the captain increasingly neglected his duties. He almost ran the Snark aground on the reefs in the Nanuku pass at the entrance to the archipelago, forcing Jack to take control and get them out of trouble.

← Martin Johnson, crew member on the *Snark*, Melanesia, June 1908.

↑ Indigenous people of Melanesia, 1908. During the *Snark*'s trip, Jack London, Charmian London or Martin Johnson took the photographs.

First page of Chapter XVI of *The Cruise of the Snark* manuscript (New York, The Macmillan Co., 1911): "Bêche de Mer English." In this chapter, Jack London explains how bêche-de-mer, a dialect mixing local words and English words, is used for trade throughout Melanesia, "In the Solomons, for instance, scores of languages and dialects are spoken. Unhappy the trader who tried to learn them all. . . . A common language was necessary—a language so simple that a child could learn it."[2]

Once in the port of Suva, on the island of Viti Levu, Jack decided to leave Warren ashore and assume command of the ship himself. When *Snark* took off for the New Hebrides on June 6, 1908, he was the only one calling the shots for the first time since leaving Oakland.

At the time, the Melanesians suffered from an appalling reputation in the eyes of Westerners. Publications and travel stories invariably portrayed them as primitive, cruel and anthropophagous headhunters. Therefore, the *Snark*'s crew was on guard as they sailed into the New Hebrides archipelago.

Upon their arrival at Port Resolution, on the island of Tanna, the boat was surrounded by dozens of canoes. The crew was confronted by natives with closed faces,

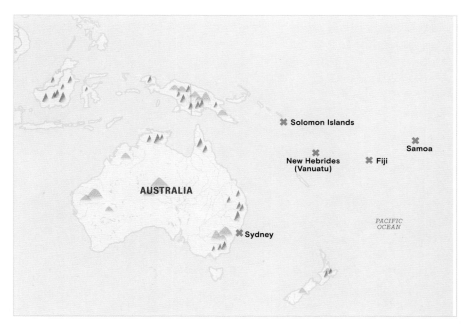

→
Henry, a member of the *Snark*
crew, at the bow of the boat,
Melanesia, 1908.

behind which the sailors perceived a deep animosity. He was also struck by their rugged and wild appearance, and their black African physiques far removed from the norms of Polynesian beauty. Charmian's comments in the logbook are edifying: "There's certainly something disjointed about it — so lovely a land and so low an order of inhabitants. . . . Bodies are thin and unbeautiful, with bulges in the wrong places; legs show thin and crooked, and their generally evil, low-browed malformed Black-Papuan faces are curiously repulsive."[3] She went on to say, "The women were deadly unfeminine — nearly resembling the men in face and voice, ageless, sexless, dirty; and they and their men displayed an ungracious hospitality."[4]

↖
Inhabitants of Melanesia, 1908 (photograph taken by Jack London, Charmian London or Martin Johnson).

↑
Indigenous people of Melanesia, Port Mary, Santa Anna Island, 1908 (photograph taken by Jack London, Charmian London or Martin Johnson).

Many natives were reluctant to let Jack photograph them. In fact, in Melanesia, racial tension was palpable everywhere, all the time. The local people were exploited on plantations—even forcibly recruited sometimes. They experienced living and working conditions that were very close to slavery. In this remote region, the explosive situation compelled whites to be very cautious, and all wore their firearms conspicuously on their belts.

Leaving Port Resolution, the *Snark* ran along Martyrs Island—named in memory of the missionaries who were there—and reached Port Vila on Elfate Island before continuing on to the Solomon Islands, which they reached June 28, 1908.

↑
Jack London (right), Charmian (next to him) and Martin Johnson (center) with Melanesian natives, 1908.

Even the climate, weighed down by foul air, had become inhospitable. The winds were violent and thunderstorms frequent. Hordes of cockroaches and mosquitoes invaded the *Snark* and oozing wounds developed from the slightest cut. All on board continually fell victim to tropical fevers. Jack was the most affected: a skin condition caused multiple ulcers, and, despite the regular application of mercuric chloride, his hands and legs peeled abnormally. Rectal wounds also caused him horrible pains and Charmian and he spent hours immersed in medical books.

"If I were king, the worst punishment I could inflict on my enemies would be to banish them to the Solomons."[5]

↑
Penduffryn plantation,
Guadalcanal, 1908.

Melanesian village, 1908
(photograph taken by Jack
London, Charmian London or
Martin Johnson).

In the Solomon Islands, the Londons made Penduffryn plantation on Guadalcanal their base. Spread over almost a square mile, it was the most important of the islands. Copra, coconut meat, was gathered and transformed into oil used in food and cosmetics. Although the island was under English control, the plantation was American. Jack and Charmian were housed in the planters' residence, a set of four large wooden buildings mounted on stilts in the heart of the jungle and surrounded by a palisade guarded day and night against a possible native revolt.

From this other-worldly backdrop, they spent several months

↖
Almost the whole *Snark* crew, Penduffryn, 1908. From left to right: Tehei (who decided after the Samoa Islands to extend his adventure); Wada; Charmian and Jack London; Martin Johnson; Harry Jacobsen and Henry.

↑
The two owners of the Penduffryn plantation: George Darbishire and Tom Harding, Guadalcanal, 1908.

↗
Costume party organized at Penduffryn plantation (Jack London is in the center, Charmian is on his left and Martin Johnson sits in the foreground), Guadalcanal, 1908.

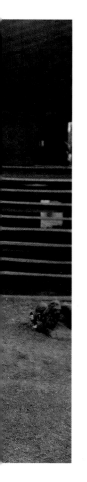

exploring the different islands of the archipelago: Malaita, where they discovered the
tiny coral villages of Langa-Langa; Santa
Isabel, where they had to careen the *Snark* to
rid her hull of the innumerable shelled crea-
tures that weighed her down; Lua-Nua, where they dropped anchor
for the first time in the heart of an atoll. They even pushed the
Snark to Tasman Island, Papua New Guinea.

   The Londons also spent some time on the ketch *Minota*,
which was commissioned to recruit natives from various villages

**"To look at, they were
certainly true head-
hunting cannibals."**[6]

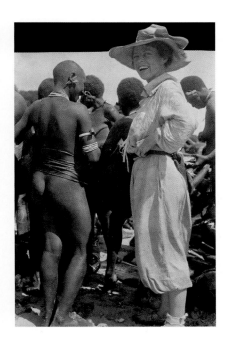

↑
Residents of a village
in the Solomon Islands,
1908 (photograph
taken by Jack London,
Charmian London or
Martin Johnson).

←
Charmian London on
a Malaita Island beach,
Solomon Islands, 1908.

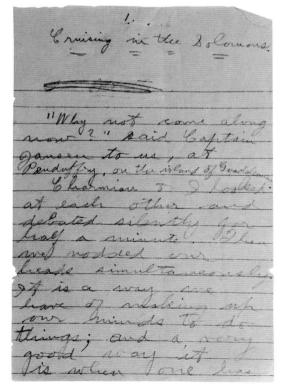

THE "MINOTA" THROWN UP ON THE REEF.

Cruising in the Solomons

By Jack London

Author of "Martin Eden," "Call of the Wild," "White Fang," etc.

[Concluded]

MORNING found us still vainly toiling through the passage. At last, in despair, we turned tail, ran out to sea, and sailed clear around Bassakanna to our objective, Malu. The anchorage at Malu was very good, but it lay between the shore and an ugly reef, and while easy to enter, it was difficult to leave. The direction of the southeast trade necessitated a beat to windward; the point of the reef was wide-spread and shallow; while a current bore down at all times upon the point.

Mr. Caulfield, the missionary at Malu, arrived in his whale-boat from a trip down the coast. A slender, delicate man he was, enthusiastic in his work, level-headed and practical, a true twentieth-century soldier of the Lord. When he came down to this station on Malaita, as

THE ISLAND OF AUKI, BUILT UP FROM THE SEA BY THE SALT-WATER MEN.

←
First page of Chapter XV of *The Cruise of the Snark*: "Cruising in the Solomons" in which Jack London recounts his journey, on Captain Jansen's *Minota*, to recruit workers from different islands in the Solomon archipelago for the Penduffryn plantation.

←
First publication of Chapter XV of *The Cruise of the Snark*: "Cruising in the Solomons" in *Pacific Monthly*, July 1910. The first pages of the chapter were published in the June issue.

↑
The *Minota*, tasked with
recruiting workers for the
Penduffryn plantation,
Solomon Islands, 1908.

↑
Melanesian natives aboard
the *Minota*, 1908.

↗
Jack London on the *Minota*'s
bridge, Solomon Islands, 1908.

and take them back to the plantation. For this dangerous mission, the ship's side rails were shielded with barbed wire, and a sentinel was permanently posted on the bridge. Jack and Charmian experienced one of the most grueling moments of their journey when, in Malu Bay, the ship was stranded on rocks for three days. Surrounded by dozens of men armed with bows, clubs and spears, only the intervention of the crew of another boat, the *Eugenie*, which had been alerted by a missionary, saved them.

The health of the *Snark*'s crew steadily deteriorated in the Solomon Islands as a result of malaria, dysentery and ngari-ngari, an infection caused by contact with tropical plants. "During all these months in the Solomons the *Snark* has been a hospital ship," Jack recalled. "We have all had the fever more times than we like to remember, as well as half a score of worse afflictions. The Japanese cook and one Tahitian sailor went crazy."[7] Worse, Jack's toes, fingers and hands, covered with ulcers, continued to peel and swell dramatically. He struggled to catch a rope or grab his pen to write even one word. Even walking had become difficult.

Realizing that his condition required serious medical care, Jack decided to temporarily interrupt their trip. On November 4, 1908, after anchoring the *Snark* near Penduffryn, he boarded the steamship *Makambo* for Sydney, accompanied by Charmian and Martin Johnson.

At St. Malo Hospital in Sydney, doctors were not able to diagnose Jack's skin ulcers: "The Australian specialists agreed that the malady was non-parasitic, and that, therefore, it must be nervous."[8]

It would take years for him to finally learn, through much reading, that exposure to the sun of the tropics was the true cause of his illness. Moreover, on November 30, he was operated on for a

Adventure

Jack's stay on the island of Guadalcanal inspired *Adventure* (New York, The Macmillan Co., 1911). The novel takes place on the Berande plantation, similar in every respect to Penduffryn. When the natives revolt, the owner, David Sheldon, falls seriously ill. Then Joan Lackland, a beautiful and young American, arrives and courageously organizes their defense.

MARTIN JOHNSON
The Traveling Companion of
JACK LONDON
And Scenes From His Wonderful
SOUTH SEA ISLAND
TRAVELOGUES

Martin Johnson

Originally chosen from hundreds of other candidates to become *Snark*'s cook, Martin Johnson (1884–1937) was the only member of the crew to complete the cruise. He recounted their adventures in the book *Through the South Seas with Jack London* (New York, Dodd, Mead & Co., 1913), as well as at lectures with projected photos of the trip. He later became one of the pioneers of documentary filmmaking and returned to Melanesia in 1917 to shoot a series of films (*Among the Cannibal Isles of the South Pacific, Cannibals of the South Seas* and *Head Hunters of the South Seas*).

double fistula. With a heavy heart, he realized that he had no choice but to end his cruise around the world.

After arranging for the *Snark* to be taken to Sydney to be sold, the Londons traveled to Tasmania for one month of convalescence pending their departure from Oceania.

Even if it ended prematurely and dramatically, this odyssey in the South Seas remained one of the Londons' most magnificent adventures. Witness this dedication by Charmian, which opened *The Log of the Snark*, published in 1915: "To MY HUSBAND who made possible these happiest and most wonderful pages of my life."[10]

↑
Natives of the Solomon Islands approaching the *Minota*. Note the barbed wire that surrounds the deck, 1908.

The South Seas significantly inspired Jack's literary output, leading him to write dozens of articles, along with a whole series of short stories and novels: *Adventure*; *The Cruise of The Snark*; *South Sea Tales*; *A Son of the Sun*; *The House of Pride*; *On the Makaloa Mat*; *Michael, Brother of Jerry*; *Jerry of the Islands*.

Some of the *Snark*'s crew continued to be a part of the Londons' lives for a long while: Nakata, the young ship's mate from Hawaii, remained their faithful servant for many years; Martin Johnson, who became one of the pioneers of documentary filmmaking, met with them regularly and even visited them on their California ranch.

The fate of the *Snark* would be much more somber—she finished up as a slave ship. Jack gave her up for $4,500; she had cost Jack seven times that.

Although still weak, Jack wanted to stop over in Latin America on the way back to California. On April 7, 1909, he, Charmian and Nakata boarded the steamship *Tymeric* bound for Ecuador. The crossing lasted 43 days and allowed them to come close to the famous island of Pitcairn, where the mutineers of the *Bounty* once took refuge. From the port of Guayaquil, they then traveled to the capital, Quito. They made this trip by rail, on a line considered at the time as "the most dangerous of the world" opened less than a year prior. Two hundred and eighty miles long, it crossed the Andes Mountains on the flanks of Chimborazo volcano at an altitude of 12,000 feet.

"It did not mend, and it was impossible for me to continue the voyage."[9]

↖
Snark careened on Santa Isabel Island to clean her hull, Solomon Islands, 1908.

↓
A bedridden Jack London on the Penduffryn plantation, Guadalcanal, 1908.

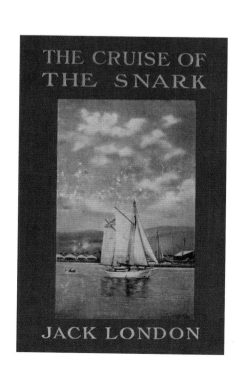

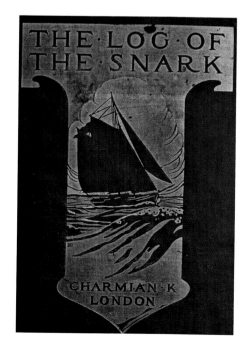

Charmian and Jack London in Tasmania, 1909.

→

Original covers of *The Cruise of the Snark* by Jack London, and *The Log of the Snark* (both New York, The Macmillan Co., 1915) by Charmian London.

↑
Jack and Charmian on the
Tymeric's bridge, bound for
South America, 1909.

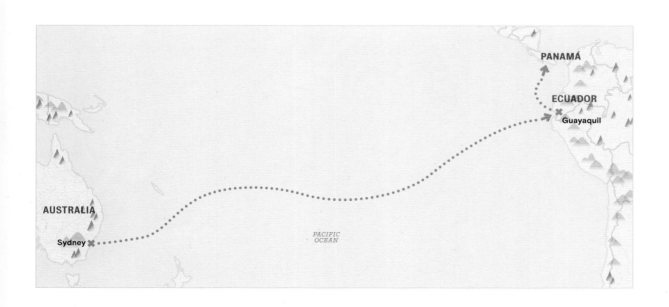

Their stay in Ecuador lasted a month, during which they hunted caiman on the Rio Guayas and attended a bull fight that Jack, indignant, described as "coward's sport."

They then traveled by boat to the young republic of Panama. Six years earlier, the country had gained independence from Colombia, thanks in particular to the support of the United States, which financed the rebellion. The Americans even dispatched a warship, the SS *Nashville*, to the area to dissuade Colombia from carrying out reprisals against the rebels. For Washington, the stakes were high: Panama was the site of the transoceanic canal project, originated by Frenchman Ferdinand de Lesseps at the end of the 19th century. For the sum of $50 million and payment of an annuity, the United States received the guarantee from the

↑
Railway line crossing the Andes to connect Guayaquil to Quito, 1909 (photograph by Jack London).

new government that the work would continue on the canal for the US, and that the US would obtain the right of exploitation of the canal and control of a zone five miles wide on each side. In the implicit economic war they were waging against the European colonial powers, the US considered Central America, the Caribbean and North America as their "preserve." Since 1823, the Monroe Doctrine condemned all intervention in the "Americas" and, in 1904, the Roosevelt Corollary further hardened this position, justifying the use of force, as had happened in Nicaragua and Honduras. Controlling the Panama Canal meant controlling the commercial activity and transportation of raw materials throughout the region and also the ability to move troops quickly from one ocean to another.

↖
Quito market, Ecuador, 1909 (photograph by Jack London).

↗
A street in Quito, Ecuador, 1908 (photograph by Jack London).

→ Charmian London on a street in Quito, Ecuador, 1908 (photograph by Jack London).

↑
The Panama Canal breaking
through Culebra Mountain,
April 8, 1907. Jack London went
to the site on July 2, 1909.

Arriving in Panama on June 25, Jack went to Culebra on July 2 to visit the canal construction site, where he marveled at the American engineers' know-how. The work site was vast — 48 miles long, monumental locks and even an artificial lake to maintain the water level. Two days later, the Londons celebrated American Independence Day in the city of Panama, before embarking for New Orleans and ultimately taking a train to their California home.

↓
Caricature published in *Puck* humor magazine, August 13, 1903, titled "The Pull of the Monroe Magnet": Uncle Sam, whose legs constitute a magnet on which is inscribed "United States Protectorates," attracts small characters symbolizing different Central America and South America states (Cuba, Nicaragua, Costa Rica, Honduras, Guatemala, El Salvador, Colombia). The state of Panama is already in his pocket.

BACK TO

CALIFORNIA

O n July 28, 1909, Jack and Charmian were back home, after an absence of 27 months. Thanks to California's more temperate climate, Jack quickly

"The country, though, is the best, the only natural life."[1]

regained his health, and devoted himself single-mindedly to building up the ranch. Jack's memory of his adoptive father John London's unfulfilled dream of exploiting his own farm was still very much alive. He made the dream his own: "I see my farm in terms of the world, and I see the world in terms of my farm,"[2] he said to Charmian. He acquired several surrounding properties, bringing his total holdings to more than 1.5 square miles, where he cultivated orchards and vineyards. He started growing, and investing in, eucalyptus—he planted 100,000 plants in the space of a few months. He asked his recently divorced stepsister, Eliza, to join him as ranch manager.

In this peaceful little paradise protected from the hustle and bustle of the city, Jack and Charmian wanted to start a real family.

←
Jack on the deck of the *Roamer* in San Francisco Bay, between 1910 and 1913.

↑
Plowing fields on Jack and Charmian London's ranch in the Valley of the Moon, circa 1911.

Just two months after returning from the South Seas, Charmian became pregnant, and Jack was thrilled to be a father again.

On June 19, 1910, a terrible event annihilated their hopes: after a difficult birth, their daughter Joy died, aged only 38 hours. The couple was devastated. Jack, who had begun writing a new novel, *The Assassination Bureau, Ltd.*, would leave it unfinished.

Charmian required complete bed rest for several weeks at the Oakland Hospital and she pushed Jack to go to Nevada to honor a contract with the *New York Herald*. Three days after the tragedy, he went to Reno as a journalist to cover the boxing match

". . . our Joy-Baby . . . only thirty-eight hours old gone in the twilight of the morning."[3] (Charmian London).

↑
Eliza Shepard, Jack's step-sister, on the ranch, circa 1911.

↑
Jack London on the ranch,
circa 1911.

←
Construction of a barn on the
ranch, circa 1911.

James J. Jeffries defeated by Jack Johnson on July 4, 1910, in Reno, Nevada: "In all the contests of [boxing's] long history, no two comparable giants have ever locked in combat."[4]

Jack London (second row, fifth from right) with other sports journalists, Reno, Nevada, July 1910.

between Jack Johnson and James Jeffries for the title of world heavyweight champion.

Jack was a knowledgeable expert respected by the most accomplished champions and regularly reported on boxing, his favorite sport. Since his early years, he had trained regularly—even with Charmian!—and always traveled with a pair of gloves, ready to respond to any challenge. According to Jack, boxing "... grew as our very language grew. It is an instructive passion of race. It is the fact, the irrefragable fact. We like fighting—it's our nature."[5] "They want to see fights because of the old red blood of Adam in them that will not down. It is a bit of profoundly significant human phenomena. No sociologist nor ethicist who leaves this fact out can cast a true horoscope of humanity."[6]

The announcement of the Reno event ignited America. "Never in a war, at any one place, was congregated so large a number of writers and illustrators,"[7] said Jack. And the disappointment was crushing when the black Johnson won with a K-O in the 16th round, annihilating the hopes of the majority of the public and experts of a victory for their "white champion." "The greatest battle of the century was a monologue delivered to twenty thousand spectators by a smiling negro who was never in doubt and who was never serious for more than a moment at a time,"[8] Jack wrote in the *New York Herald*.

After losing their child, it was sailing—as so often in their lives—that brought Jack and Charmian a little respite. Jack bought a 30-foot sailboat, the *Roamer*, on which they would regularly cruise for weeks at a time around the Bay. Together with Nakata, the young Hawaiian ship's boy from the *Snark*, they explored the deltas of the Sacramento and San Joaquin rivers, where they caught catfish and hunted wild ducks. They also visited Jack's old

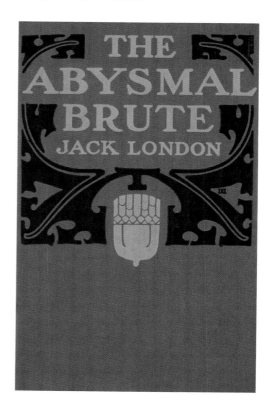

Jack London wrote many short stories around boxing, including "The Mexican," "The Game" and "The Abysmal Brute." In the latter, he denounced the exploitation of professional boxers by their managers and fight organizers.

acquaintances from the oyster pirate days: Charley Le Grant, a former fishing patrol agent; and the ex-pirate French Frank. "What a blissful passage it was, this first *Roamer* voyage," Charmian remembered, "only to be surpassed by the second and the third, and so on. As Jack said, 'Snarking' once more."[10]

"Once a sailor, always a sailor. The savor of the salt never stales."[11] Jack explained that at Glen Ellen, "I am the sailor on horseback!"[12]

On the *Roamer*, Jack and Charmian drew up plans for their next big project: to build, in the heart of Glen Ellen, a monumental house where they would live from then on.

Called Wolf House, it would be built on a large floating slab, able to withstand the severest earthquakes. Combining a rustic appearance with the most modern and refined facilities, it also had to integrate in perfect harmony with surrounding nature. Its walls were made of blocks of lava stone, its frame consisted of giant redwood trunks and its roof covered with Spanish tiles.

"I have turned rancher, and live beyond sight of the sea. Yet I can stay away from it only so long. After several months have passed, I begin to grow restless."[9]

↓
The *Roamer*,
circa 1910.

↖
The *Roamer*, circa 1910.

↑
Jack London with French
Frank, the former oyster pirate,
Vallejo, 1911.

→
Charmian London with
French Frank, Vallejo, 1911.

←
Jack at the helm of the
Roamer, circa 1910.

↗
Jack London hunting wild duck
on the *Roamer*, circa 1910.

→
Nakata on board the *Roamer*,
circa 1910.

→
"Together we came to know
the rivers and serpentine
sloughs, with their foreign
inhabitants, as Jack had known
them aforetime"[13] (Charmian
London).

Everything was oversized in the Wolf House: with a total surface area of 48,000 square feet, it included three buildings, arranged around a central patio housing an outdoor pool, fed by a mountain spring; It contained 26 rooms, spread over four stories, with nine large chimneys; it was equipped with a ventilation system, hot water and electricity that supplied both lighting and heating.

Everything was planned to allow the couple to be separate or together, depending on how they felt: Jack's room was perched at the top of the building, above Charmian's apartment; to write, he had a vast office connected by a spiral staircase to a library of the same size, where all his documents were finally together; the double living room accommodated Charmian's Steinway grand piano.

Other rooms were designed for housing staff, for recreation or for meditation. And the many visits by friends and acquaintances inspired specific spaces, including guest rooms and an enormous dining room capable of receiving 50 guests.

The work on Wolf House was to last for many months, so the couple moved nearby to an old restored cottage.

While waiting for their new home to be built, Jack and Charmian decided to embark on a new adventure: during the summer of 1911, with Nakata still by their sides, they journeyed 1,500 miles through northern California and Oregon in a carriage pulled by four horses.

After ascending the Pacific coast, they traversed the still wild mountains lined with thousand-year-old redwoods, and stopped in small isolated towns where their arrival always caused a sensation. "We went to see where history had been made, and we saw scenery as well . . . every turn bringing into view a picture of breathless beauty; every glance backward revealing some perfect composition in line and colour, the intense blue of the water margined with splendid oaks, green fields, and swaths of orange poppies."[16]

"My house will be standing, act of God permitting, for a thousand years."[14]

←
Jack at the Wolf House building site, 1912.

↓
Drawing of the Wolf House, made by San Francisco architect Albert Farr, around 1910.

↑
Wolf House: almost finished,
1913.

↗
Jack on the construction site,
examining the Wolf House
plans, 1913.

→
The cottage Jack and
Charmian London lived in
during the work on Wolf House,
around 1913.

In search of his roots in this America of another age, Jack tried to experience the emotion felt by the first pioneers: "I am a Westerner, despite my English name. I realize that much of California's romance is passing away, and I intend to see to it that I, at least, shall preserve as much of that romance as is possible for me."[17]

"Having selected Sonoma Valley for our abiding place, Charmian and I decided it was about time we knew what we had in our own county and the neighbouring ones."[15]

→
Jack and Charmian
London on their trip
through California
and Oregon,
summer 1911.

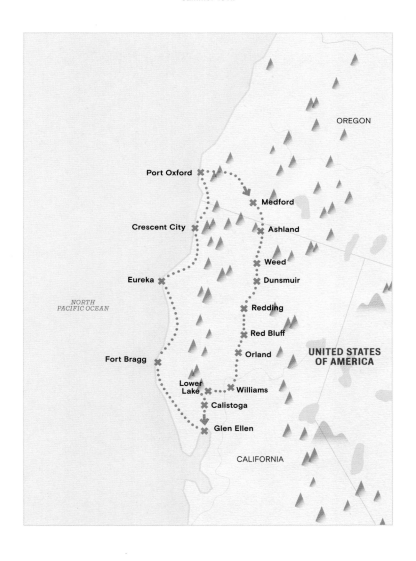

← Jack London at a stop in the forest, summer 1911. "To him relaxation consisted not in cessation but in change of thought and occupation"[18] (Charmian London).

↗ "What man has done, I can do . . . And please don't forget that when we sailed on the *Snark* I knew nothing of navigation, and that I taught myself as I sailed."[19]

→ "From Glen Ellen to the Coast, and north to Bandon, Oregon, was our route"[20] (Charmian London).

THE DARK

HOURS

Glen Ellen became the place to re-energize between two adventures. Barely a few months after their horse and carriage trip through northern California, Jack and Charmian embarked on a long cruise aboard a four-masted Cape-Horner, the *Dirigo*. The ship was not allowed to take on passengers, so, though they paid for their trip, they had to "officially" become crewmembers, Jack as a third mate and Charmian as stewardess. Nakata, who traveled with them, was "assistant steward."

The *Dirigo* left Baltimore March 2, 1912, and sailed south along the US coast to Cape Horn, before reaching the port of Seattle, Washington. Onboard, Jack and Charmian remained cut off from the world for 148 days.

As usual, the Londons wrote, read, played cards and boxed. They also observed the ship's operations, and discovered, from

"In all the one hundred and forty-eight days, our eyes rested on land but once. . . . literally land's end, the end of the earth, the island of Cape Horn itself, with the continuous mainland."[1] (Charmian London).

←
Jack on his ranch in the Valley of the Moon, around 1913.

↑
Charmian London on the bridge of the *Dirigo*. She holds in her arms the fox terrier Possum, bought in New York before embarking, and who would from then on be their faithful companion, 1912.

Next double page: The *Dirigo*, 1912. "Enough and bitter cold it was, but nothing mattered to me except the fact that land was left behind, in prospect long months of blissful sea life with its cleansing simplicities"[2] (Charmian London).

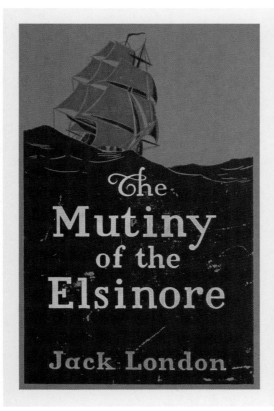

The Mutiny of the *Elsinore*

With the documents he had onboard the *Dirigo*, Jack London wrote his novel *The Mutiny of the Elsinore* (New York, The Macmillan Co., 1914). The book's protagonist, Galbraith, is a wealthy writer. Unhappy and discouraged, he embarks in Baltimore on a Cape-Horner leaving for Valparaiso, accompanied by his Japanese valet and his fox terrier. The captain's young middle-class daughter, Margaret, is also traveling aboard the *Elsinore*. Galbraith quickly falls in love with her. But the ship is plagued by strong social tensions: the captain rules the crew of vagrants and convicts with an iron hand. The author describes them as brutes and drunkards, on the brink of pure animality. When the revolt breaks out, Galbraith manages to contain the mutineers at the front of the ship with his hunting rifle. Hungry and vanquished, they end up surrendering.

As he went through terrible hardships in his life—deterioration of his health, the collapse of his dream of becoming a father again, running after money—Jack London wrote his darkest book. The pessimistic tone was already indicated in the name he chose to give the ship, borrowed from the city where Shakespeare's tragedy Hamlet takes place. Survival of the fittest prevails in *The Mutiny of the Elsinore*, and the ruling class, ruthless and without mercy, domineers in the end, keeping the disinherited in their clutches. "The tang of power!" exclaims Galbraith at the end of the novel. "I was minded to let literature get the better of me and read the rascals a lecture; but thank heaven I had sufficient proportion and balance to refrain."[3]

the inside, how sailors lived their daily lives. Upon their arrival in Seattle, Martin Johnson, their former *Snark* companion, came to greet them. They learned with dismay that the *Titanic* had just sunk off Newfoundland, and that the former Ecuadorian president and leader of the revolution, José Eloy Alfaro Delgado, who they met during their stay in Quito, had been lynched by a raging crowd.

During their cruise, Charmian became pregnant again. A week after returning to the ranch, she miscarried, at the age of 39. Both understood then that the ideal home they had built would remain, despite their deepest desire, childless.

At Glen Ellen, Jack's dreams for his land seemed to know no bounds. He meticulously studied the latest agricultural technical journals and was constantly launching ever more ambitious projects. In 1913, he paid a premium price for Neuadd Hillside, a prize-winning draft horse weighing in at one ton. To store his corn, he began the construction of two 50-foot silos, the first in California to be made of cement.

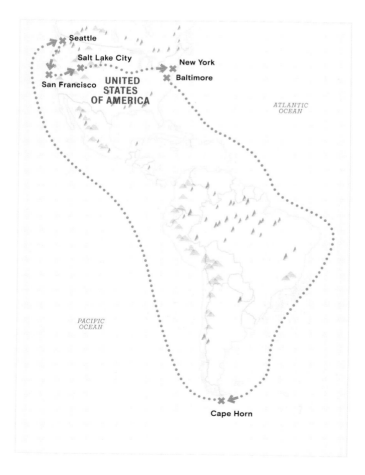

Dirigo's sailors at work, 1912
(photograph by Jack London).

The *Elsinore* raced on through the storm-white sea and the wrath-somber sky

The Sea Gangsters

A MODERN TALE OF LOVE, MUTINY AND FATE ABOARD THE GOOD SHIP "ELSINORE."

By Jack London

Author of "The Call of the Wild," "Smoke Bellew," "John Barleycorn," etc.

Illustrated by Anton Otto Fischer

SYNOPSIS: Out from Baltimore, down across the Four Seas swings the good ship *Elsinore*, under can- they could knock seamanship into them. And he proceeded to do it, literally. Right then and there

↖
Prepublication of the novel
The Mutiny of the Elsinore
under the title "The Sea
Gangsters," in *Hearst's
Magazine*, January 1914.

←
Dirigo's sailors at work, 1912
(photograph by Jack London).
"Jack chose the *Dirigo* over
a much newer clipper for
the reason that she carried
skysails fast becoming
obsolete"[4] (Charmian London).

→
Illustration by Anton Otto
Fischer for the prepublication
of the novel *The Mutiny of the
Elsinore* in *Hearst's Magazine*,
1914.

The ranch had become a real money pit. He had to pay for the staff, maintenance of the lands, new investments. Jack was constantly strapped for cash, and fought endless legal battles to prevent the fraudulent use of his books. He also had to negotiate mortgages with banks and advances with his various publishers on a regular basis. Novels, short stories, articles; he wrote relentlessly, becoming a veritable slave, condemned to write for life.

During 1913, a series of dramatic events altered all areas of his life. His fruit crops were destroyed by frost, and the eucalyptus trees were ravaged by a swarm of grasshoppers. As his debts mounted, bad investments further exacerbated his financial situation. The altercations with Bessie, his ex-wife, had escalated. Love gave way to hatred between the two former spouses: she was constantly asking for more money and turning his daughters, Joan and Becky, against him.

Since the separation, Bessie had refused to let their children visit Jack on the ranch, and to see them, he had to meet them in Oakland, for a meal in a restaurant, a movie or a walk in Idora park. For Jack, the impossibility of intervening in their education gave rise to unbearable frustration. Everything went against the bourgeois and Puritan vision that Bessie, subject to the conventions of the time, tried to convey to their daughters: "I refuse further," Jack wrote to her, "to sacrifice all of my father-love and interest in order to satisfy the narrow prejudice of your narrow mind."[10] Joan, the eldest, sided with her mother. Misunderstanding was real, conflicts were frequent and abundant

"There is so much developing I want to keep on doing, endless experiments I want to make."[5]

↗
Jack and his magnificent stallion, at Glen Ellen Ranch, around 1913. "Jack founded his pure-bred English Shire stable by the purchase of nothing less than Neuadd Hillside, grand champion of California, and once prize-winner in England"[6] (Charmian London).

→
Jack drew on Chinese traditional methods for farming: "What am I doing? In a few words I am trying to do what the Chinese have done for forty centuries, namely, to farm without commercial fertilizer. I am rebuilding worn-out hillside lands that were worked and destroyed by our wasteful California pioneer farmers."[7]

↑
Jack in front of the first ranch silo, 1913.

←
The first silo on the ranch, built by Jack, Glen Ellen, 1913. "A concrete-block silo, twelve feet in diameter, the first of two, and the first of their kind in California, was rising half a hundred feet into the air near the old cowbarns"[8] (Charmian London).

↑
Jack in front of the cottage,
Glen Ellen, around 1913.
"Oh, I shall make mistakes
a-many; but watch my
dream come true. . . . Try to
realize what I am after."[9]

↗
Jack in his office, Glen
Ellen, circa 1911.

correspondence testifies, page after page, to the gulf that continued to widen between them. In February 1914, during a violent crisis, Jack wrote his daughter these terrible words: "Years ago I warned your mother that if I were denied the opportunity of forming you, sooner or later I would grow disinterested in you, I would develop a disgust, and that I would turn down the page. . . . Now, do not make mistake of thinking that I am now running away from all filial duties and responsibilities. I am not. . . . I shall take care of the three of you. You shall have food and shelter always. But,

"I am so tired of writing that I'd cut off my fingers and toes in order to avoid writing."[11]

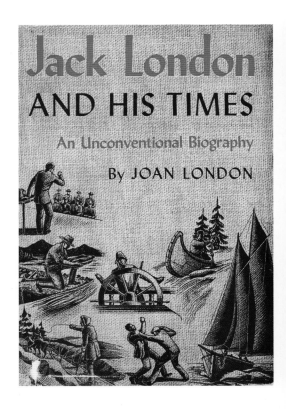

unfortunately, I have turned the page down, and I shall be no longer interested in the three of you."[12]

Alcohol, which he had consumed since his early years, also plunged Jack into frequent depressions. Charmian was increasingly intolerant of his drinking excesses, which usually took place in the company of his artist friends, such as the poet George Sterling. To protect his marriage, he practiced complete abstinence during the months spent on the *Dirigo*.

In the autobiographical *John Barleycorn*, Jack felt the need to confess his addiction to alcohol with the utmost sincerity: "It is a habit of mind to which I have been trained all my life. It is now part of the stuff that composes me. I like the bubbling play of wit, the chesty laughs, the resonant voices of men, when, glass in hand, they shut the grey world outside and prod their brains with the fun and folly of an accelerated pulse."[14]

The book was a huge public success and became the flagship of the temperance leagues. Six years later, the temperance movement won its case when prohibition—which Jack encouraged—was decreed throughout the country.

Too much alcohol, certainly. But too much tobacco, as well, too many troubles, too

Joan London (1901–1971),
Jack's eldest daughter,
published several books. Two
of them are about her father:
*Jack London and His Times:
An Unconventional Biography*
(New York, Doubleday, Doran
and Company, Inc., 1939) and
Jack London and his Daughters
(Berkeley, Heyday Books,
1990), an unfinished memoir,
published after her death.

←
Jack with Becky and Joan,
circa 1910.

↑
Joan and Becky, Jack's two
daughters, Oakland, circa 1904.

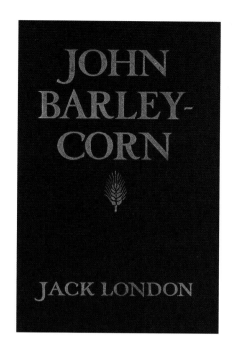

JOHN BARLEY-CORN

JACK LONDON

Published Weekly

The Curtis Publishing Company
Independence Square
Philadelphia

London: 5, Henrietta Street Covent Garden, W.C.

THE SATURDAY EVENING POST

Founded A°D¹ 1728 *by* Benj. Franklin

Copyright, 1913, by The Curtis Publishing Company in the United States and Great Britain

Entered at the Philadelphia Post-Office as Second-Class Matter

Entered as Second-Class Matter at the Post-Office Department Ottawa, Canada

Volume 185　　　PHILADELPHIA, MARCH 15, 1913　　　Number 37

JOHN BARLEYCORN

I Was Sent From the House, Half a Mile Away, to Carry Him a Pail of Beer

By JACK LONDON

ILLUSTRATED BY H. T. DUNN

IT ALL came to me one election day. It was on a warm California afternoon, and I had ridden down into the Valley of the Moon from the ranch to the little village to vote Yes or No to a host of proposed amendments to the constitution of the state of California. Because of the warmth of the day I had several drinks before casting my ballot and divers drinks after casting it. Then I had ridden up through the vineclad hills and rolling pastures of the ranch and arrived at the farmhouse in time for another drink and supper.

I had several drinks before casting taste. It had been painfully acquired. Alcohol had been a dreadfully repugnant thing— more nauseous than any physic. Even now I did not like the taste of it. I drank it only for its "kick." And from the age of five to that of twenty-five I had not learned

I outlined my life to Charmian and expounded the makeup of my constitution. I was no hereditary alcoholic. I had been born with no organic, chemical predisposition toward alcohol. In this matter I was normal in my generation. Alcohol was an acquired

much of everything . . . As he approached his 37th year, Jack's state of health had deteriorated terribly, and his body, once so vigorous, began to betray him: "In my jaw are cunning artifices of the dentists which replace the parts of me already gone. Never again will I have the thumbs of my youth. Old fights and wrestlings have injured them irreparably. . . . The joints of the legs that bear me up are not so adequate as they once were, when, in wild nights and days of toil and frolic, I strained and snapped and ruptured them."[16]

Jack knew that, physically, he was a different man, and his wonderful adventures were now a thing of the past. "Never again can I swing dizzily aloft and trust all the proud quick that is I to a single rope-clutch in the driving blackness of storm," he avowed

> **"*John Barleycorn* is not fiction at all. It is bare, bald, absolute fact, a recital of my own experiences in the realm of alcohol."[13]**

in the final pages of *John Barleycorn*. "Never again can I run with the sled-dogs along the endless miles of Arctic trail."[17]

In July 1913, while he was hospitalized for an appendicitis operation, the doctors discovered that his kidneys were in a dismal state. This situation produced chronic uremia that ate away at him little by little, and he was condemned to a death sentence in the medium term without a severe dietary regimen.

Barely a month later came the worst disaster of that horrible year. Work on Wolf House was almost complete, and Jack and Charmian planned to move there in the early days of fall. But on August 22, around midnight, a fire broke out. The spontaneous combustion of oily rags left there by workers was probably the origin of the first flames. In a few hours, the framework blazed and the roof collapsed. In the morning, after the fire had burned violently for six hours, all that remained were the walls.

Beyond the financial disaster, something broke in Jack, forever: "It isn't the money loss, though that is grave enough just at this time. The main hurt comes from the wanton despoiling of so much beauty."[18]

"My position on alcohol is absolute nationwide prohibition. I mean absolute."[15]

". . . flames and smoke rose straight into the windless, star-drifted sky"[19] (Charmian London).

"My face changed forever in that year of 1913. It has never been the same since."[20]

Next double page: Wolf House after the terrible fire of August 22, 1913.

LONDON FILMS

I n 1913, anxious to broaden his audience and diversify his revenue sources, Jack joined the nascent film world. At the time, movies were silent and often inspired by literary works in order to take advantage of the popularity of their authors. They were shot mostly outdoors, and Jack's books, rich in colorful characters and action scenes in wild settings, were perfect for adaptation to the screen.

His first cinematographic experience took place in 1908 on the Penduffryn plantation in the Solomon Islands. Three operators from Pathé were shooting a film—now lost—and Jack enjoyed playing the role of the plantation owner, who was killed in a cannibal attack.

The arrival of a personality such as Jack's in the fledgling cinema industry caused a sensation, as evidenced by these lines

←
Jack on his Glen Ellen
ranch, 1913.

↑
The Pathé team Jack met on
the Penduffryn plantation, his
first contact with the film world,
Guadalcanal, 1908.

written by a reporter after an interview given by the writer in New York, the January 31, 1914: "I have never seen more eloquent eyes than the bluish grey pair that looked out of London's head. They shine with the virtues of plain living and high thinking and they gleam with the light of genius. The entrance of such a man into the field of motion pictures is surely a good sign of the times and a matter of congratulation between all friends of the higher ideals in the world of the screen."[2]

Hollywood did not exist in those years. Independent producers settled on the West Coast because of the climate, certainly, but they also wanted to escape the stranglehold on the industry by the Edison Company, which held the initial patents. While the films produced were essentially short films of one or two reels, the first feature films were emerging, for example, *From the Manger to the Cross*, the life of Jesus Christ, released in 1912 and *Quo Vadis*, an Italian sword-and-sandal film released in the United States in 1913. Jack intended to negotiate overall adaptation rights for his books with a single company dedicated to the production of an ambitious collection of "Jack London Films" in feature format. However, he did not want to intervene directly in the writing and making of the films so that he could devote himself entirely to his literary work.

After an unsuccessful first partnership with the Balboa Amusement Producing Company, he eventually signed a contract with Hobart Bosworth, a well-known actor-director, associated in Bosworth Inc.

"To get the images living in my brains into the brains of others."[1]

↓
Scene from the Pathé film shot on the Penduffryn plantation and in which Jack London appeared, Guadalcanal, 1908.

with financier Frank A. Garbutt. Bosworth is often considered today as the "Dean" of Hollywood: a theater actor, he began his film career in 1908, and when he met London he had already written, directed and performed in dozens of films for the famous Selig Polyscope Corporation. He was a man of imposing physique, whose adventurer past was sure to captivate Jack: he had been, among other things, a wrestler, ranch hand and sailor on a whaling boat.

But, when Bosworth Inc. decided to start production on *The Sea Wolf*, a legal dispute arose between London and the Balboa company. The two companies then simultaneously shot two competing adaptations of the same book! Jack was furious and had to battle, in

↑
Pathé shooting on the
Penduffryn plantation,
Guadalcanal, 1908.

↑
Hobart Bosworth, producer,
director and often-principal
actor in the Jack London Films,
1914.

↗
Jack London and Frank A.
Garbutt, financier and treasurer
of Bosworth Inc., producer of
the Jack London Films, San
Pedro, 1914.

his own words, the "the hottest, hardest business fight of his life."[3] He even joined the Authors League of America to assert his rights, but had to ultimately accept an out-of-court settlement, and both versions were shown on screens at the same time.

    To clearly identify the official version of the film, approved by Jack, to the public, a short sequence was shot with him on the Glen Ellen Ranch and inserted at the beginning of the film, with the mention "Jack London Films. " In the spirit of *Alfred Hitchcock Presents* . . . a few years later, prologues were made for each of the

↑
The film crew of *The Sea Wolf*, 1913. Hobart Bosworth is the fourth from the right.

following films: *Martin Eden*, 1914; *The Valley of the Moon*, 1914; *An Odyssey of the North*, 1914. In *John Barleycorn*, 1914, where three actors interpret the role of Jack at different times in his life, Jack himself appears in an epilogue: we find him on his boat, the *Roamer*, followed by the heading "And this is my message."[4] Moreover, in the advertising material provided to exhibitors and film magazines, Bosworth Inc. left no room for doubt: "We are the only authorized producers in motion pictures of all Jack London's literary work, past, present and future."[5]

When the Londons attended the first public screening of *The Sea Wolf* at San Francisco's Grauman's Imperial Theater on October 5, 1913, they were thrilled with Bosworth's performance as the horrible Captain Larsen: "Mr. Hobart Bosworth, the real, three dimension, flesh-and-blood Sea Wolf," exclaimed Jack. "Until I die the image of the Sea Wolf will be Mr. Bosworth as I saw him on the screen."[8]

Hobart Bosworth in *The Sea Wolf*, 1913. "Until I die the image of the Sea Wolf will be Mr. Bosworth as I saw him on the screen."[6]

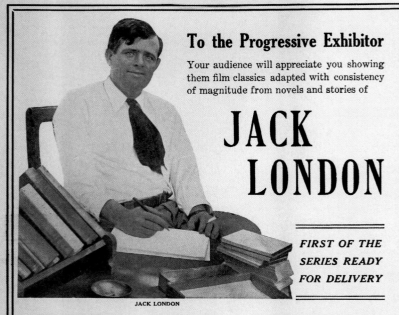

To the Progressive Exhibitor

Your audience will appreciate you showing them film classics adapted with consistency of magnitude from novels and stories of

JACK LONDON

JACK LONDON

FIRST OF THE SERIES READY FOR DELIVERY

THE SEA WOLF

IN SEVEN REELS

Typically characteristic of the author himself; redolent with the tang of the salt sea; a story that lays bare men's brute passions, yet portrays with exquisite touch the most original character in modern fiction.

Wire or write us for particulars of our exclusive territory contract for the first twelve Jack London productions

BOSWORTH
INC.

EXECUTIVE OFFICES
648 South Olive St., Los Angeles, Cal.

SALES DEPARTMENT
110 West 40th Street, New York City

MENU

"BARLEYCORN" COCKTAILS CAPE COD

"BURNING DAYLIGHT" CELERY   OLIVES AU "SEA WOLF"

"MARTIN EDEN" PUREE

CHICKEN CASSEROLE AU "VALLEY OF THE MOON"

POTATOES "PARAMOUNT"

HEARTS OF ROMAIN "LONDON" DRESSING

"BOSWORTH" NEAPOLITAN PARFAIT

ASSORTED CAKES "ODYSSEY"

CAFE AU "PHANTOM"

SMOKES

CIGARS "SMOKE BELLEW"
CIGARETTES "HYPOCRITES"

Advertisement for the version of *The Sea Wolf* produced by Bosworth Inc., published in the *Motion Picture News*, December 20, 1913. In the dispute against the Balboa company, the producer of another film adaptation of the same book said, "Jack had gone into the fight with every atom of his energy, and, since his downfall would mean that of all American authors, he was backed, should he lose, by the Authors' League of America, in the determination to carry the fight into the highest courts of the Union"[7] (Charmian London).

Menu of a dinner given by Bosworth Inc. to Philadelphia journalists to promote Jack London Films, held at the Adelphia Hotel on September 23, 1914. Each of the dishes alluded to Jack London and his works: "Barleycorn" cocktails, "Burning Daylight" celery, olives of the "Sea Wolf," "Martin Eden" puree, "Valley of the Moon" chicken, hearts of romaine with "London" dressing . . . And for the end of the meal "Smoke Bellew" cigars!

Jack and Charmian thought that the film would be the first in a long series of successes. However, it was not to be, much like the hope for enormous profits. Despite major publicity, Jack London Films, apart from *The Sea Wolf*, received at best mixed critical and public reactions.

Most of these films have now disappeared and it is difficult to fully understand the reasons for this failure. Rereading the reviews of the time and the correspondence between Jack and Bosworth Inc., it appeared that Hobart Bosworth's acting, too respectful of the literary work, certainly lacked rhythm. "Some of our productions, artistically and expensively produced, do not have the drawing power that other and flashier productions have at the present time,"[10] admitted financier Frank A. Garbutt. Jack himself was certainly aware of the dangers of remaining too faithful to his works. From the beginning, he gave his producers artistic carte blanche: "Take all the liberty in

Herbert Rawlinson (Humphrey van Weyden) and Hobart Bosworth (Captain Wolf Larsen) in the movie *The Sea Wolf* (1913), adapted from the novel published in 1904. In August 1913, Jack and Charmian were on set for the first takes, shot in San Francisco Bay: "It was the beginning of the picturing of my stuff, and the first time I've ever seen moving pictures made, and I had one of the best times of my life."[9] The film was released on December 7, 1913, two months before Charlie Chaplin made his first appearance on screen in the short film "Making a Living," produced by Mack Sennett for Keystone Studio.

the world with my text. To follow my text literally, I deemed would not make popular, from moving-picture standpoint."[11] He had also repeatedly drawn attention to the need to clarify the stories, using more inter-titles: "We cannot be too high-brow with our ordinary commonplace moving picture audiences and cannot depend too much upon their imagination to bridge the gap and . . . Few people of the average moving picture audience had never read nor heard of the story that they are seeing and trying to grasp for the time on the screen."[14] And when East Coast exhibitors blamed the movie endings for being too dramatic and confusing audiences, Jack, again, encouraged distance from the original work: "I do not see any reason why the scenario writer could not change the story so as to accomplish happy endings instead of tragic endings. Please know that in this matter of freedom to the scenario writer of changing any of my endings or conclusions that I give a free fist."[15]

↖
"What a vista of discoveries in the unseen world stretches before the mind as it contemplates the power of the motion picture in the field of education. . . . The motion picture will help to unlock many doors. I think every thing with the possible exception of demonstrations in political economy will eventually go through the hands of the filmer."[12]

↑
Herbert Rawlinson, Hobart Bosworth and Viola Barry (Maud Brewster) in *The Sea Wolf* (1913). "Now I have become hugely interested in the motion pictures, I am getting the habit, I am beginning to study them and learning to tell the difference between the good and the bad. Yes, I thought that the screen was all right for landscapes, events, etc., but of its real might I had no idea."[13]

Jack Conway (Billy) and
Myrtle Stedman (Saxon)
in *The Valley of the Moon*
(1914). "Throughout we find
fine film renderings of Jack
London's best points, his
intimate revelations with
their autobiographic vein,
his marvelous powers of
description and the spirit of
poetry and romance in which
he treats of the modern and
the commonplace" (*The Moving
Picture World*, August 29, 1914).

The Valley of the Moon was
released in June 1914. The
exterior shots were taken at
Glen Ellen in December 1913.

Advertisement for the film *The
Valley of the Moon* in *Moving
Picture World*, August 29, 1914.

Several other factors seemed to have played a role as well: censorship, which watered down Jack's works, notably amputating many scenes of drunkenness from *John Barleycorn* and a scene of rioting workers from *The Valley of the Moon*; the length of the feature films when nickelodeon audiences were used to programs of short films; the small rooms that needed to be redesigned; and, finally the war, which had just been declared in Europe and effectively disrupted the distribution of films outside the United States.

The Jack London Films, ambitious precursors in many ways, certainly suffered from the period in which they were made. The film industry was, at that moment, extremely vibrant, and 1914 marked the birth of Hollywood: the studios quickly amassed all power—production, distribution, exploitation—and independent producers were pushed to the side. In open conflict with his financier, the millionaire Frank A. Garbutt, Hobart Bosworth joined Universal to begin a new acting career. Garbutt, meanwhile, decided to stop the production of Jack London Films, considered unprofitable, and to join in with Paramount to develop entertainment films, built around the new stars of the screen.

This incursion into the 7th art left Jack with a bitter taste in his mouth; that of financial failure, of course, but also the memory of the endless legal fighting to defend his copyrights and his inability to really control the production and distribution processes, because he was too busy with his travels and numerous other activities.

Jack London will "reap a fortune from the production of his stories in moving picture form"[16] (Hobart Bosworth).

He tried a final collaboration with Hearst's Cosmopolitan Pictures, but it did not produce any results. No other adaptation of his works came out on the screens during his lifetime.

Most of the Jack London Films made by Bosworth have disappeared. Only the film *Martin Eden*, released August 16, 1914, starring Lawrence Peyton in the title role and Viola Barry as his great love Ruth Morse, along with some reels of the film *An Odyssey of the North* have survived.

"All my stuff which had been produced had proved a financial failure and had earned me nothing."[17]

→
John Barleycorn (1914).
"*John Barleycorn*, by Jack London, created a tremendous sensation when it appeared as a serial story in the *Saturday Evening Post*, and will appear in book form simultaneously with the film production. This is a most unique production, being practically a life confession of the early struggles of the author with King Alcohol" (*Motion Picture News*, December 13, 1913).

↗
In *John Barleycorn* (1914), actor Antrim Short played Jack London as a young writer.

John Barleycorn (1914). Concerning the scene in which the young Jack London (played by Matthew Robert) was forced to drink wine by his Italian neighbors, the Pennsylvania State Board of Censors demanded: "Reduce drinking scene at Italian picnic. Eliminate caption about boy's fear of Italians."[18]

BOSWORTH
INC.
PRESENTS

JOHN BARLEYCORN

BY

JACK LONDON

DIRECTED BY
HOBART BOSWORTH

6 REELS 6

HANDLED EXCLUSIVELY BY THE
Progressive Motion Picture Co.
645 Pacific Building, San Francisco, Cal.
FOR THE ENTIRE WESTERN TERRITORY

John Barleycorn and the censors

Cover of a promotional booklet for *John Barleycorn* sent to movie exhibitors, 1914.

Adapted from the book in which Jack London confesses his alcoholism, *John Barleycorn* sparked unquestionable controversy. While a referendum was scheduled for the public to decide on possible prohibition, companies connected to the alcohol trade, worried about the film's impact, put pressure on producers to reschedule its release. Rejecting an offer of $25,000, Bosworth Inc. put *John Barleycorn* on the market in July 1914, with the support of the Women's Christian Temperance Union, which considered the film as

"the strongest moral argument against drink ever offered to the public in motion picture form."[19]

But the censors in Ohio and Pennsylvania blocked the film; they demanded cutting many scenes and shooting new scenes to show, at the end, "the man's true reformation."[20]

Famous Players Exchange, responsible for the film's distribution, braved the ban and programmed *John Barleycorn* at Philadelphia's Garrick Theater. Despite threats of arrest, nearly 2,500 people rushed there the first two nights. Finally, after a legal and media battle in which the close ties between the chief motion

picture censor of Pennsylvania and the liquor lobby are revealed, the film was released in that state in August 1914, with many fewer cuts required and without additional scenes shot.

An Odyssey of the North, a film adapted from Jack London's 1900 novel, was released on US screens on September 3, 1914. Hobart Bosworth plays the role of Naas, a mixed-blood Inuit searching for his wife-to-be, who was kidnapped by a white sailor on their wedding day.

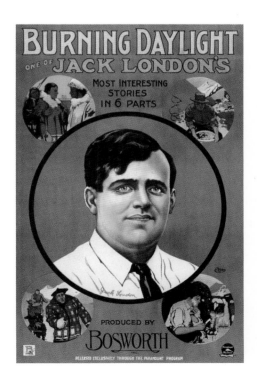

↑
Hobart Bosworth (Elam
Harnish, nicknamed Burning
Daylight) and Myrtle Stedman
(Dede Mason) in *Burning
Daylight*, 1914.

→
Burning Daylight movie poster,
released September 14, 1914.
The film featured two major
episodes: *Burning Daylight:
The Adventures of Burning
Daylight in Alaska*, and *Burning
Daylight: The Adventures of
Burning Daylight in Civilization*.

THE CHECHAKO
BEING SOME OF THE ADVENTURES OF "SMOKE BELLEW"
JACK LONDON

↑
Jack Conway (Christopher
Belliou, aka Smoke Bellew) and
Myrtle Stedman (Joy Gastell)
in *The Chechako*, adapted
from Jack London's *Smoke
Bellew*, published in 1912.
Faced with the lack of success
of the Jack London Films,
Paramount canceled the film's
release, originally scheduled
for November 23, 1914. Hobart
Bosworth failed in an attempted
to sell the film to Universal.
The Chechako was never
distributed. [21]

The Chechako, 1914.

↑

The Chechako, 1914. The Klondike
exterior scenes were filmed in
Truckee, northern California,
during the winter of 1913–1914.
When the members of Bosworth's
team arrived there on February 1,
1914, "They found eight feet of
snow on the level, fences being
entirely submerged, and drifts
hiding the eaves of some of the
houses. Several storms since
have given welcome opportunity
for work in falling snow . . . The
company's trained Alaskan dogs
went wild with delight when they
found themselves in the snow
again" (*Motion Picture World*,
March 21, 1914).

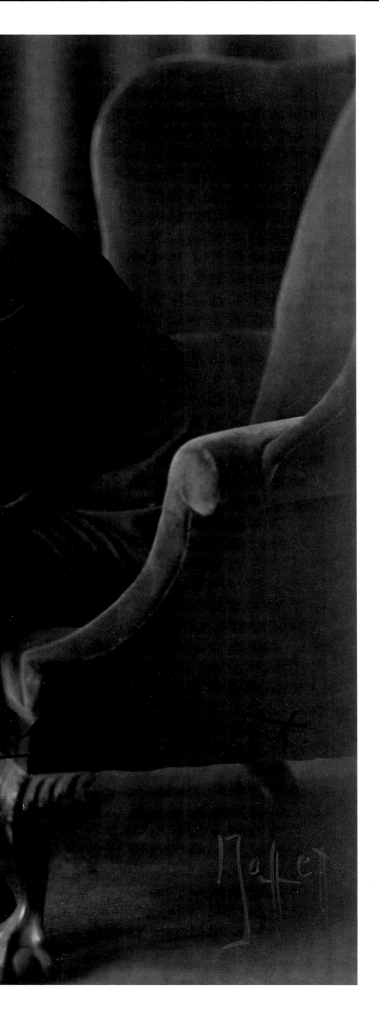

←
Hobart Bosworth with Skookum, the dog he used for the three adaptations of Jack London's works inspired by the Far North: *An Odyssey of the North*, *Burning Daylight* and *The Chechako*. Bosworth bought Skookum in Alaska (along with many malamutes and huskies for the movies) and became very fond of him. When filming ended, the dog became his faithful companion and accompanied him to California, where he was presented in public several times.

THE END

OF THE ROAD

erpetually indebted by work on his ranch and the financial support of his family, Jack was condemned to continue writing. He maintained his thousand words a day, working indifferently on works of fiction or articles for the press.

In April 1914, he accepted a proposal from *Collier*'s magazine to go to Mexico as a war correspondent and report on the recent intervention of American naval forces in Veracruz.

This event marked an important date in the history of diplomatic relations between the two countries. For years, the United States had supported the regime of dictator Porfirio Díaz, who was favorable to their many investments in the country. When the revolution broke out in 1910, Americans largely controlled the oil fields, mines and railways, and owned more than 25 percent of the land in Mexico. Worried about destabilization of the region and having its interests questioned, the American government cautiously supported the constitutionalist Francisco Madero, who came to power in 1911 thanks to free elections. But the country remained divided. Madero did not come through with the hoped-for reforms

←
Jack and Charmian London
between 1915 and 1916.

↑
Jack and Charmian aboard the
Kilpatrick, Veracruz, 1914.

"Dear, brave comrades of the Mexican Revolution."[1]

and lost the support of the other revolutionaries, Pancho Villa, Emiliano Zapata and Venustiano Carranza. He was assassinated during a coup and the country fell into the hands of Victoriano Huerta, who established a new military dictatorship in February 1913. While rebellion was rife throughout the country, Washington refused to recognize this new power and tried by all means to subvert it. The American government suspended all economic aid, mobilized troops along the border and declared an arms embargo. In 1914, it was just a matter of waiting for a pretext to intervene militarily.

Two successive events would provide what they needed: on April 9, nine sailors from an American whaler entered territorial

↑
American troops in
Veracruz, 1914 (photograph
by Jack London).

↗
Jack London (second from left)
with other war correspondents
in Veracruz, 1914.

waters to get fuel and were arrested in Tampico. Huerta released them 24 hours later, but President Woodrow Wilson found the Mexican's excuses inadequate and sent several Navy ships into Mexican waters. Hearing that a cargo of 15,000 cases of arms—chartered by the American merchant Remington and transported via Odessa and Hamburg—was to be delivered to Huerta by a German steamer in the port of Veracruz, Wilson directed the fleet towards that city. Veracruz was bombed, the Marines stormed in and martial law decreed. This incident immediately triggered anti-American demonstrations in other cities around the country and throughout Latin America. Many American nationals had to be evacuated and repatriated to Texas or Louisiana where refugee camps were set up.

Jack London arrived in Veracruz on April 27 aboard the troop transport *Kilpatrick* along with other war correspondents. Most of the military operations were finished. During his one-month stay, he wrote seven major articles, in which he described in detail the movements of the American army and the effects of the conflict on the civilian population. And, on a trip to Tampico, he met prisoners of war held at San Juan de Ulúa prison and constitutional rebels.

A few years earlier, London had shown passionate support for those whom he called his "Dear, brave comrades of the Mexican Revolution," and his socialist friends naturally expected him to condemn the American

intervention. But, to their surprise, Jack agreed with the government's stance: "American occupation gave Vera Cruz a bull market in health, order, and business . . . Verily, the Vera Cruzans will long remember this being conquered by the Americans, and yearn for the blissful day when the Americans will conquer them again."[2] Jack believed the revolution had gone on too long and the country needed order, which only the United States was able to provide: "The big brother can police, organize, and manage Mexico. The so-called leaders of Mexico cannot. And the lives and happiness of a few million peons, as well as of many millions yet to be born, are at stake."[3]

He attacked the Spanish mestizos, a "class that foments all the trouble, plays childishly with the tools of giants, and makes a shambles and a chaos of the land."[4] He often reduced the Mexican revolutionaries to mere bandits who, "in this sad, rich land, steal pay rolls of companies and eat out hacienda after hacienda as they

Charmian London in the company of American officers at San Juan de Ulúa prison, Veracruz, 1914 (photograph by Jack London).

Mexican prisoners detained in San Juan de Ulúa, Veracruz, 1914 (photograph by Jack London).

picnic along on what they are pleased to call wars for liberty, justice, and the square deal." [5]

Jack also denounced the miserable conditions of the peasants, often forcibly conscripted into the armies of the revolution: "[The soldier] is not fighting for any principle, for any reward. It is a sad world, in which witless, humble men are just forced to fight, to kill, and to be killed. The merits of either banner are equal, or, rather, so far as he is concerned, there are no merits to either banner." [6] But if his texts bear witness to a real empathy for the poorest segments of the Mexican population, exploited and perpetually maintained in a state of poverty, they also demonstrate manifest racism and reflect the general feeling of North Americans toward their southern neighbors, judged lazy, uneducated and violent.

At the end of May, Jack was overcome by a bout of dysentery that confined him to his hotel room, fighting death. Terribly

↑
Mexican prisoners detained in San Juan de Ulúa, Veracruz, 1914 (photograph by Jack London).

weakened, he had to be evacuated, and was finally back in Glen Ellen by the middle of June.

American forces, meanwhile, remained in Veracruz for many months. They left on November 23, once an agreement had been reached between the two countries under the arbitration of Argentina, Brazil and Chile. This episode may have precipitated the fall of Victoriano Huerta, but it also deteriorated relations between Washington and Mexico. In 1916, the United States launched another military intervention, this time by land, to pursue Pancho Villa and his men. And the following year, discovering that Germany had proposed an alliance with Mexico by guaranteeing the return of its former possessions—Texas, Arizona and New Mexico—President Woodrow Wilson decided to involve the United States in the First World War.

Veracruz marked, for Jack, a decisive step in his 20-year relationship with the Socialist Party. His articles were perceived as treason, and his former comrades accused him of being paid by American oil executives to defend their interests. A few months later, the situation worsened when they also reproached him for his commitment to American intervention in Europe, to which they remain firmly opposed. In Jack's eyes, faced with the German danger, the armed struggle was inevitable: "I am a profound pro-ally. I believe that the present war is a war between civilization and barbarism, between democracy and oligarchy."[7]

The split between Jack and the other American socialists was final. The writer accused the party of lacking courage and accepting too many compromises. He resigned on March 7, 1916.

At Glen Ellen, Eliza continued to run the ranch and carry on with Jack's grand projects for the farm.

Although busy with his literary work and his many travels, Jack was able to increase

←
Mexican constitutionalist, Tampico, 1914 (photograph by Jack London).

↗
Jack London in his hotel room, Veracruz, 1914 (photograph by Charmian London).

→
Covers of *Collier's* magazines containing two of Jack London's articles detailing the events in Veracruz: "The Red Game of War" (May 16, 1914) and "Mexico's Army and Ours" (May 30, 1914).

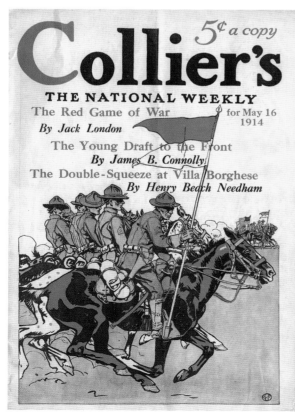

the area of the estate to 1,500 acres in barely 10 years. He built a dam to irrigate the land and created an artificial lake in which he introduced 1,500 catfish. He raised angora goats, Jersey bulls and cultivated grapes, grains and fruit trees, for which he refused to use industrial fertilizers and instead studied Chinese traditional methods at great length. He also built a pigsty so modern that people in the area called it the "Pig Palace."

His health, however, continued to deteriorate: uremia and kidney stones were frequent occurrences, and his body, prematurely aged, was marked by disease. At the beginning of 1915, he and Charmian decided to go to Hawaii to relax for a while. After visiting the World

"I am resigning from the Socialist Party because of its lack of fire and fight, and its loss of emphasis on the class struggle. "[8]

↑
Jack and Charmian (first row, left) with friends in Hawaii, between 1915 and 1916.

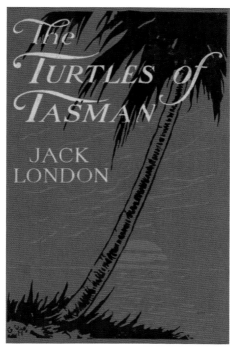

←
Jack London in Hawaii, between 1915 and 1916. "All during these last months of his life, there was in Jack the widening gratification that he was advancing in his conquest of the heart and understanding of the people of Hawaii, Hawaii-born Anglo-Saxon and part Hawaiian, and the ever dear and dearer Hawaiians themselves"[9] (Charmian London).

↑
Original cover of The Turtles of Tasman collection, The Macmillan Co. The book, published in September 1916, was the last of Jack London's works to be published during his lifetime. The main character of the short story, Tom, returns home after an adventurous life led all around the world. He is a generous man who fascinates everyone who approaches him. When he dies, one of his friends has this to say: "He was a man."[10] But is Jack still talking about his character or about himself? Predictably, the last story in the collection is entitled "The End of the Story."

Expo in San Francisco—which commemorated the reconstruction of the city following the 1906 earthquake—and attending the recent inauguration of the Panama Canal, they embarked on the steamship *Matsonia*, on February 24, headed for Honolulu.

The Londons had not returned to the Hawaiian Islands since the end of the *Snark*'s journey, and this visit lasted five months. Apart from writing, their time was mainly spent bathing, napping and reading aloud on the shore. They returned again at the end of 1915, this time for seven months. They felt at home in Hawaii, where they had known the happiest times of their lives; they even thought of making the archipelago their new home. Jack spent hours observing the Hawaiians surfing, a "royal sport," according to him, "intended for the natural Kings of earth." He was given the title of *kamaaina*: one who was not born there, but who Hawaiians considered one of theirs.

↖
Jack and Charmian in Hawaii, between 1915 and 1916. "They were happy hours, lying on the shady sand among the barbaric black-and-yellow canoes, reading aloud, napping, and chatting with our friends. Later in the day we swam through and beyond the breakers and spent some of the most wonderful moments of our united lives"[11] (Charmian London).

↑
Young surfers in Hawaii. From his first visit to these islands during the *Snark*'s voyage, Jack London had had a passion for the sport: ". . . to-morrow, ah, to-morrow! I shall be out in that wonderful water, and I shall come in standing up. . . . And if I fail to-morrow, I shall do it the next day, or the next. Upon one thing I am resolved: the *Snark* shall not sail from Honolulu until I, too, wing my heels with the swiftness of the sea, and become a sun-burned, skin-peeling Mercury."[12]

During the summer of 1916, Jack immersed himself in publications covering the nascent field of psychoanalysis. This new discipline had appeared 20 years previously and was organized around the Viennese Psychoanalytic Society, founded by Sigmund Freud and his followers. Jack was fascinated by Carl Gustav Jung, whose European practice was highly regarded across the Atlantic and attracted many wealthy American patients as well. Jung, who was just a year older than Jack, examined the creative process among artists, writers and musicians alike. *Psychology of the Unconscious*, published in 1913, deeply affected Jack. It showed him how to understand the motivations of his deepest being by taking a fresh look at his work and his personal journey. "I am standing on

"'See Naples, and die' — they spell it differently here: see Hawai'i and live."[13]

↑
Jack and Charmian in Hawaii between 1915 and 1916.

Jack London at his office, Hawaii, 1915. "Through successive visits, including eighteen months spent in the Islands during the last two years of his life, through early misunderstanding and final loving comprehension of him, Jack London and Hawaii have drawn together, with increasing devotion in his heart for 'Aloha-land'—'Love-land' in his fashion of speech—until at the end he could answer to the long-desired appellation, 'kamaaina,' one-who-belongs, and more"[14] (Charmian London).

"My Hawaiian Aloha," a three-part article published in *Cosmopolitan* in September, October and November 1916: "Somehow, the love of the Islands, like the love of a woman, just happens. One cannot determine in advance to love a particular woman, nor can one so determine to love Hawaii. One sees, and one loves or does not love. With Hawaii it seems always to be love at first sight."[15]

Jack London   39

My Hawaiian Aloha

By Jack London

EDITOR'S NOTE—This is the second of Mr. London's articles on our delightful territorial possession—Hawaii. The first appeared in the September issue.

HAWAII is the home of shanghaied men and women, and of the descendants of shanghaied men and women. They never intended to be here at all. Very rarely, since the first whites came, has one, with the deliberate plan of coming to re-

Good-by, proud California!" and departed. Now he was a poet, with an eye and soul for beauty, and it was only to be expected that he would lose his heart to Hawaii as Mark Twain and Stevenson and Stoddard had before him. So he came, with his wife and garden hose and rake and hoe. Heaven alone knows what preconceptions he must have entertained. But the fact remains that he found naught of beauty and charm and delight. His stay in Hawaii, brief as it was, was a hideous nightmare. In no time, he was *(Continued on page 142)*

Waterfall in the Kohala Mountains, Hawaii

Ditch-trail on a Hawaiian mountainside

main, remained. Somehow, the love of the Islands, like the love of a woman, just happens. One cannot determine in advance to love a particular woman, nor can one so determine to love Hawaii. One sees, and one loves or does not love. With Hawaii, it seems always to be love at first sight. Those for whom the Islands were made, or who were made for the Islands, are swept off their feet in the first moments of meeting, embrace, and are embraced.

I remember a dear friend who resolved to come to Hawaii and make it his home forever. He packed up his wife, all his belongings, including his garden hose and rake and hoe, said,

Hawaiian girl playing the *ukulele*—a native guitar which has become popular in this country

Daughters of Hawaii

the edge of a world so new, so terrible, so wonderful," he told Charmian, "that I am almost afraid to look over into it."[17]

But disease left him no respite. When they left for California, at the end of July 1916, his kidneys had practically ceased functioning and caused him intense pain. At only 40 years old, Jack had put on a lot of weight and could not ride or even swim. His upper teeth had fallen out, and he had to wear dentures. He suffered from stomach cramps and rheumatism; his temperament became more difficult and mood swings were frequent.

He died November 22, 1916 on his ranch in the Valley of the Moon, following a bout of uremia.

Four days later, in the presence of Charmian, his stepsister Eliza and a few relatives, his ashes were placed under a stone of the Wolf House, as he had wished.

"No word stirred the hush. No prayer, for Jack London prayed to no God but humanity. The men, uncovered, reverent, stood about among the trees, and when their senior had risen, the stone was rolled into place"[16] (Charmian London).

→
Original cover of *Our Hawaii* (New York, The Macmillan Co., 1917), written by Charmian London and published after Jack's death as evidence of their relationship to this archipelago.

← Jack and Charmian London with their dog Possum, a few days before Jack's death, Glen Ellen, November 1916.

→ Jack London, a few days before his death, November 1916. "There was that in his face which brought me white nights, and caused his friends to ask, 'What ails Jack? He looks well enough, but there's something about him . . . his eyes. . . .'"[18] (Charmian London).

→ Jack London in the "Pig Palace," November 1916. Photogram taken from the film shot on the ranch by a team from Pathé six days before his death. "The 'piggery' which Jack invented . . . became famous the world over, not only among farmers but with curious laymen as well. Entirely of rock and concrete, it is on a circular plan, surrounding, with graveled driveway between, a handsome tower wherein feed is mixed and distributed to the 'suites' of apartments"[19] (Charmian London).

Next double page: Charmian London on the veranda of Glen Ellen cottage three years after Jack's death. Charmian spent a lot of time with Eliza keeping the ranch running. She also wrote a long, two-volume biography of London and spent the rest of her life maintaining his memory, supervising his writings and their adaptations to the screen. She died on June 14, 1955, nearly 40 years after Jack's death. At her request, her ashes were placed with his, in the Valley of the Moon.

To Jack London

Cover of the special edition of *Overland Monthly*, entirely dedicated to Jack London, published in May 1917. In the opening pages was a poem by George Sterling, written in tribute to his old friend and entitled "To Jack London":

Oh, was there ever face, of all the dead,
In which, too late, the living could not read
A mute appeal for all the love unsaid—
A mute reproach for careless word and deed?
And now, dear friend of friends, we look on thine,
To whom we could not give a last farewell, —
On whom, without a whisper or a sign,
The deep, unfathomable Darkness fell.
Oh! Gone beyond us, who shall say how far?
Gone swiftly to the dim Eternity,
Leaving us silence, or the words that are
To sorrow as the foam is to the sea.
Unfearing heart, whose patience was so long!
Unresting mind, so hungry for the truth!
Now hast thou rest, O gentle one and strong,
Dead like a lordly lion in its youth!
Farewell! although thou know not, there alone.
Farewell! although thou hear not in our cry
The love we would have given had we known.
Ah! And a soul like thine—how shall it die?[20]

NOTES

FOREWORD
A SUPERB METEOR

1. *Jack London, By Himself*, New York, The Macmillan Co., 1913, n.p.
2. Quoted by Russ Kingman in *A Pictorial Life of Jack London*, New York, Crown Publishers, Inc., 1979.
3. Arnold Genthe, quoted by Jeanne Campbell Reesman and Sara S. Hodson, *Jack London, Photographer*, Athens: University of Georgia Press, 2010.

1876–1893
SAN FRANSISCO BAY

1. "What Life Means To Me," *Cosmopolitan Magazine*, March 1906.
2. *John Barleycorn*, New York, The Century Co., 1913.
3. "Small-Boat Sailing," *Yachting Monthly*, August 1912.
4. *John Barleycorn*. op. cit., p. 62.
5. "What Life Means To Me," *Cosmopolitan Magazine*, op. cit., p. 21.
6. *John Barleycorn*, New York, The Century Co., 1913.
7. *A Pictorial Life of Jack London*, New York, Crown Publishers, Inc., 1979, p. 29.
8. *John Barleycorn*, op. cit.
9. Ibid.
10. "That Dead Men Rise Up Never," in *The Human Drift*, New York, The Macmillan Co., 1917.
11. "Story of a Typhoon Off the Coast of Japan," *The San Francisco Morning Call*, November 12, 1893.

1893–1897
CONFRONTING UNRESTRAINED CAPITALISM

1. *Revolution*, New York, The Macmillan Co., 1910.
2. *The Road*, New York, The Macmillan Co., 1907, p. 131.
3. N/A
4. *The Road*, op. cit., p. 48.
5. Ibid., p. 134.
6. Ibid., p. 90.
7. *Revolution*, op. cit., p. 219.
8. "How I Became a Socialist," *The Comrade*, March 1903.
9. Ibid., p. 360.
10. *Revolution*, op. cit., p. 221.
11. *The Star Rover*, New York, The Macmillan Co., 1915, p. 389.
12. *Revolution*, op. cit., p. 49.
13. *A Pictorial Life of Jack London* by Russ Kingman, New York, Crown Publishers, Inc., 1979.
14. Ibid., p. 56.
15. *John Barleycorn*, New York, The Century Co., 1913, p. 180.
16. Ibid., p. 172.
17. "How I Became a Socialist," art. cit., p. 358.
18. Ibid., p. 360.
19. Ibid., p. 359

1897–1902
ADVENTURES IN THE FAR NORTH

1. *Smoke Bellew*, New York, The Century Co., 1912.
2. *A Daughter of the Snows*, New York, J.B. Lippincott Co., 1902.
3. *Jack London, By Himself*, New York, The Macmillan Co., 1913.
4. Russ Kingman, *A Pictorial Life of Jack London*, New York, Crown Publishers, Inc., 1979, p. 68.
5. "The White Silence," in *The Son of the Wolf*, Boston, Houghton, Mifflin Co., 1900.
6. Russ Kingman, *Jack London*, op. cit., p. 67.
7. Quoted by Charmian London, *The Book of Jack London*, New York, The Century Co., 1921, p. 238.
8. *Martin Eden*, New York, The Macmillan Co., 1909, p. 111.
9. Russ Kingman, op. cit.
10. *John Barleycorn*, p. 181.
11. Ibid., p. 146.
12. Ibid.

1902–1904
CELEBRATED AUTHOR

1. *The People of the Abyss*, New York, The Macmillan Co., 1903, p. 33.
2. Ibid., p. 174.
3. Ibid., p. 181.
4. Ibid., p. 29.
5. *The People of the Abyss*, New York, The Macmillan Co., 1903, p. 89-90.
6. *Martin Eden*, New York, The Macmillan Co., 1909, p. 406.
7. *The Call of the Wild*, New York, The Macmillan Co., 1903, p. 142.

1904
WAR CORRESPONDENT

1. "Japan's Invasion of Korea, As Seen by Jack London," *The San Francisco Examiner*, March 4, 1904.
2. Russ Kingman, *A Pictorial Life of Jack London*, New York, Crown Publishers, Inc., 1979, p. 129.
3. "Japanese Officers Consider Everything a Military Secret," *The San Francisco Examiner*, June 19, 1904.

1904–1906
THE VALLEY OF THE MOON

1. *The Valley of the Moon*, New York, The Macmillan Co., 1913, p. 355.
2. Ibid., p. 527.
3. Letter from Jack London to George Brett, December 5, 1904, in *The Letters of Jack London, Vol. 1: 1896-1905*, Stanford University Press, 1988.
4. Charmian London, *The Book of Jack London*, New York, The Century Co., 1921, p. 102.
5. Closing Jack London often used when corresponding with friends.
6. Russ Kingman, *A Pictorial Life of Jack London*, New York, Crown Publishers, Inc., 1979, p. 135.
7. Ibid., p. 135.
8. Ibid.
9. *The Strength of the Strong*, New York, The Macmillan Co., 1914, p. 44.
10. Review of "The Jungle," *The Wilshire Magazine*, August 1906.

1906–1907
AND THE EARTH SHOOK...

1. "The Story of an Eye Witness," *Collier's*, May 5, 1906.
2. Ibid.

1907–1908
ACROSS THE PACIFIC

1. *The Cruise of the Snark*, New York, The Macmillan Co., 1911, p. 74.
2. Ibid., p. 64.
3. Ibid., p. 123.
4. Ibid., p. 131.
5. Ibid., p. 123.
6. *Martin Eden*, New York, The Macmillan Co., 1909, p. 256.
7. *The Cruise of the Snark*, op. cit., p. 66.
8. Ibid., p. 28.
9. Charmian London, *The Log of the Snark*, New York, The Macmillan Co., 1915, p. 173.
10. Ibid., p. 186.
11. *The Log of the Snark*, op. cit., p. 175.
12. Ibid., p. 184.
13. Quoted by Charmian London, *The Log of the Snark*, op. cit.

1908–1909
THE BLACK ISLANDS

1. *The Cruise of the Snark*, New York, The Macmillan Co., 1911.
2. Ibid., p. 234.
3. Charmian London, *The Log of the Snark*, New York, The Macmillan Co., 1915, p. 177.
4. Ibid., p. 181.
5. *The Cruise of the Snark*, op. cit., p. 223.
6. Ibid., p. 211.
7. Letter from Jack London to George Sterling, October 31, 1908, in *The Letters of Jack London, Vol. 2: 1906-1912*, Stanford University Press, 1988, p. 770.
8. *The Cruise of the Snark*, op. cit., p. 264.
9. Ibid.
10. Charmian London, *The Log of the Snark*, op. cit., p. 11.

1909–1911
BACK TO CALIFORNIA

1. *Jack London, By Himself*, New York, The Macmillan Co., 1913, n.p.
2. Jack London, quoted by Charmian London *in The Book of Jack London*, New York, The Century Co., 1921, p. 266.
3. Charmian London, *The Book of Jack London*, op. cit., p. 189.
4. "Crowning Fight of Ring's History, says Jack London," *The New York Herald*, July 2, 1910.
5. "Ape and Tiger in U.S. Demand Fight, says Jack London," *The New York Herald*, June 29, 1910.
6. "Jack London Says Reno Crowds Eagerly Await Big Fight Because of 'Old Red Blood of Adam That Will Not Down,'" *The New York Herald*, June 24, 1910.
7. Ibid.
8. "Negro, Never in Doubt, Fear or Trouble, Played All the Time, says Jack London," *The New York Herald*, July 5, 1910.
9. "Small-Boat Sailing," in *Yachting Monthly*, August 1912.
10. Charmian London, *The Book of Jack London*, op. cit., p. 198.
11. "Small-Boat Sailing," art. cit.
12. Jack London, cited by Charmian London in *The Book of Jack London*, op. cit., p. 26.
13. Charmian London, *The Book of Jack London*, op. cit., p. 199.
14. Jack London, quoted by Charmian London in *The Book of Jack London*, op. cit., p. 102.

15. "Navigating Four Horses North of the Bay," *Sunset Magazine*, September 1912.
16. Ibid.
17. Jack London to a Sacramento journalist, quoted by Charmian London in *The Book of Jack London*, op. cit., p. 200.
18. Charmian London, *The Book of Jack London*, op. cit., p. 200.
19. "Navigating Four Horses North of the Bay," art. cit.
20. Charmian London, *The Book of Jack London*, op. cit., p. 212.

1912 – 1913
THE DARK HOURS

1. Charmian London, *The Book of Jack London*, New York, The Century Co., 1921, p. 240-241.
2. Ibid., p. 240.
3. *The Mutiny of the Elsinore*, New York, The Macmillan Co., 1914, p. 428.
4. Charmian London, *The Book of Jack London*, op. cit., p. 240-241.
5. Jack London to Charmian London, quoted in *The Book of Jack London*, op. cit., p. 266.
6. Charmian London, *The Book of Jack London*, op. cit., p. 268.
7. Letter to Geddes Smith, October 31, 1916, in *The Letters of Jack London, Vol. 3: 1913-1916*, Stanford University Press, 1988, p. 1600-1601.
8. Charmian London, *The Book of Jack London*, op. cit., p. 276.
9. Jack London, quoted by Charmian London in ibid., p. 267.
10. Letter to Bessie London, January 8, 1911, in *The Letters of Jack London, Vol. 2: 1906-1912*. Stanford: Stanford University Press, 1988, p. 970.
11. Letter to Cordie Webb Ingram, April 9, 1913, in *The Letters of Jack London, Vol. 3: 1913-1916*, op. cit., 1988.
12. Letter to Joan London, February 24, 1914, in *The Letters of Jack London, Vol. 3: 1913-1916*, op. cit., p. 1299.
13. Letter to Roland Phillips, February 27, 1913, in ibid., p. 1128.
14. *John Barleycorn*, New York, The Century Co., 1913, p. 250.
15. Telegram to Reverend W.H. Geystweit, October 6, 1916, in *The Letters of Jack London, Vol. 3: 1913-1916*, op. cit., p. 1583.
16. *John Barleycorn*, op. cit., p. 231.
17. Ibid.
18. Jack London, quoted by Charmian London in *The Book of Jack London*, op. cit., p. 262.
19. Charmian London, ibid., p. 261.
20. Jack London, quoted by Charmian London in ibid., p. 255.

1913 – 1914
THE JACK LONDON FILMS

1. "Jack London – Picture Writer," *Moving Picture World*, January 31, 1914.
2. Ibid.
3. Charmian London, *The Book of Jack London*, New York, The Century Co., 1921, p. 260
4. Tony Williams, Jack London – The Movies, an Historical Survey. Los Angeles: Davis Redjl, 1992.
5. Ad for Bosworth Inc. in *Motion Picture News*, November 8, 1913.
6. "Jack London – Picture Writer," art. cit.
7. Charmian London, *The Book of Jack London*, op. cit., p. 253.

8. Jack London, quoted by Charmian London in ibid., p. 253-254.
9. "When Jack London was amazed," *Motion Picture News*, December 6, 1913.
10. Letter from Frank A. Garbutt to Jack London, December 28, 1914, in *The Letters of Jack London, Vol. 3: 1913-1916*, Stanford University Press, 1988, p. 1403.
11. Letter to Frank A. Garbutt, May 4, 1915, in ibid., p. 1458.
12. "Jack London – Picture Writer," art. cit.
13. ibid.
14. Letter to Frank A. Garbutt, September 21, 1914, in *The Letters of Jack London, Vol. 3: 1913-1916*, op. cit., p. 1373.
15. Ibid.
16. "When Jack London was amazed," art. cit.
17. Letter to Frank A. Garbutt, December 26, 1914, in *The Letters of Jack London, Vol. 3: 1913-1916*, op. cit., p. 1402.
18. "Pennsylvania and Ohio Censors attack 'John Barleycorn' Film," *Motion Picture News*, August 1, 1914.
19. *Motography*, July 11, 1914.
20. "Pennsylvania and Ohio Censors attack 'John Barleycorn' Film," art. cit.
21. AFI (American Film Institute).

1914 – 1916
THE END OF THE ROAD

1. Open letter from Jack London to the Mexican revolutionaries, published in the *Los Angeles Citizen*, February 11, 1911.
2. Jack London, "Mexico's Army and Ours," *Collier's*, May 30, 1914.
3. Ibid.
4. Jack London, "The Trouble Makers of Mexico," *Collier's*, June 13, 1914.
5. Ibid.
6. Jack London, "Mexico's Army and Ours," art. cit.
7. Letter to John M. Wright, September 7, 1915, in *The Letters of Jack London, Vol. 3: 1913-1916*, Stanford University Press, 1988, p. 1498.
8. Letter to the Glen Ellen local section of the Socialist Party, March 7, 1916, in *The Letters of Jack London, Vol. 3: 1913-1916*, op. cit., p. 1537.
9. Charmian London, *Our Hawaii*, New York, The Macmillan Co., 1917, p. 318.
10. Jack London, *The Turtles of Tasman*, New York, The Macmillan Co., 1916, p. 56.
11. Charmian London, *The Book of Jack London*, op. cit., p. 311.
12. Jack London, *The Cruise of the Snark*, New York, The Macmillan Co., 1911 p. 89.
13. Jack London, "My Hawaiian Aloha," *Cosmopolitan*, October 1916.
14. Charmian London, *Our Hawaii*, op. cit., p. ix.
15. Jack London, "My Hawaiian Aloha," *Cosmopolitan*, October 1916.
16. Charmian London, *The Book of Jack London*, op. cit., p. 396.
17. Jack London, quoted by Charmian London in *The Book of Jack London*, op. cit., p. 323.
18. Charmian London, *Our Hawaii*, op. cit., p. 342.
19. Charmian London, *The Book of Jack London*, op. cit., p. 276-277.
20. George Sterling, "To Jack London," *Overland Monthly*, May 1917.

THE AUTHORS

MICHEL VIOTTE

Michel Viotte has made some 40 documentaries for French television.

His films, shot in different parts of the world (Africa, Greenland, Canada, USA, Central America, Australia, New Zealand, Polynesia) focus on adventure, discovery, history and artistic creation. He is the author of the book *La Guerre d'Hollywood*, published by Editions de La Martinière (2013).

SELECTIVE FILMOGRAPHY

Jack London, une aventure américaine, 2016
Frank Sinatra, ou l'Âge d'or de l'Amérique, 2015
*La Guerre d'Hollywood : Unis sous le drapeau
– Face aux dictatures – Sur tous les fronts*, 2013
La Route du Western, du Montana au Rio Grande, 2012
Maori, 2011
Histoires de jouets (avec Pascal Pinteau), 2010
*La Route du blues : De Chicago à Memphis
– De Memphis à La Nouvelle-Orléans*, 2010
Jean Malaurie, une passion arctique, 2010
Les Juments de la nuit, récit d'une création, 2010
Avignon, cour d'honneur et champs de bataille
(avec Bernard Faivre d'Arcier), 2006
Les Autres Hommes, 2006
Albert Richter, le champion qui a dit non, 2005
Louons maintenant les grands hommes, 2004
Gérard Philipe, un homme, pas un ange
(avec Gérard Bonal), 2003
Caméras sauvages, 2003
Le Dernier Safari, 2003
Le Secret des Navajos, 2002
*De Superman à Spider-Man : l'aventure
des super-héros*, 2001
Jean Gabin, gueule d'amour, 2001
Le Temps de Lumière, 2000
Les Amants de l'aventure (avec Michel Le Bris), 1999
Au pays des totems, 1999
Jay-Jay Johanson, 1999
René Goscinny, profession humoriste, 1998
Ben Harper & the Innocent Criminals, 1997
À l'abordage!, 1997
Tortuga, l'île des flibustiers, 1997
Les Anges noirs de l'utopie (avec Michel Le Bris), 1997
Jack Kerouac, un rêve américain au temps d'Hiroshima
(avec Éric Sarner), 1996
Per Jakez Hélias, le conteur des merveilles
(avec Michel Le Bris), 1996
Jack London, l'enfant secret du rêve californien
(avec Michel Le Bris), 1995
La Mémoire des terres, 1994

NOËL MAUBERRET

An authority on Jack London's work, Noël Mauberret is director of publication for the Jack London collection at Phébus publishers, and has personally translated several works by the writer. He was president of the Jack London Society from 2012 to 2014.

BIBLIOGRAPHY

JACK LONDON'S NOVELS

The Cruise of the Dazzler, 1902
A Daughter of the Snows, 1902
The Call of the Wild, 1903
The Kempton-Wace Letters, 1903
The Sea-Wolf, 1904
The Game, 1905
White Fang, 1906
Before Adam, 1907
The Iron Heel, 1907
Martin Eden, 1909
Burning Daylight, 1910
Adventure, 1911
The Scarlet Plague, 1912
A Son of the Sun, 1912
The Abysmal Brute, 1913
The Valley of the Moon, 1913
The Mutiny of Elsinore, 1914
The Star Rover, 1915
The Little Lady of the Big House, 1915
Jerry of the Islands, 1917
Michael, Brother of Jerry, 1917
Hearts of Three, 1920
The Assassination Bureau, Ltd., 1963

JACK LONDON'S SHORT STORY COLLECTIONS

Son of the Wolf, 1900
Chris Farrington, Able Seaman, 1901
The God of His Fathers and Other Stories, 1901
Children of the Frost, 1902
The Faith of Men and Other Short Stories, 1904
Tales of Fish Patrol, 1905
Moon-Face and Other Stories, 1906
Love of Life and Other Stories, 1907
Lost Face, 1910
South Sea Tales, 1911
When God Laughs and Other Stories, 1911
The House of Pride and Other Stories, 1912
Smoke Bellew, 1912
A Son of the Sun, 1912
The Night-Born, 1913
The Strength of the Strong, 1914
The Turtles of Tasman, 1916
The Human Drift, 1917
The Red One, 1918
On the Makaloa Mat, 1919
Dutch Courage and Other Stories, 1922

JACK LONDON'S AUTOBIOGRAPHICAL MEMOIRS

The Road, 1907
The Cruise of the Snark, 1911
John Barleycorn, 1913

JACK LONDON'S NON-FICTION AND ESSAYS

Through the Rapids on the Way to the Klondike, 1899
From Dawson to the Sea, 1899
What Communities Lose by the Competitive System, 1900
The Impossibility of War, 1900
Phenomena of Literary Evolution, 1900
A Letter to Houghton Mifflin Co., 1900
Husky, Wolf Dog of the North, 1900
Editorial Crimes — A Protest, 1901
Again the Literary Aspirant, 1902
The People of the Abyss, 1903
How I Became a Socialist, 1903
The War of the Classes, 1905
The Story of an Eyewitness, 1906
A Letter to Woman's Home Companion, 1906
Revolution, and Other Essays, 1910
Mexico's Army and Ours, 1914
Lawgivers, 1914
Our Adventures in Tampico, 1914
Stalking the Pestilence, 1914
The Red Game of War, 1914
The Trouble Makers of Mexico, 1914
With Funston's Men, 1914

WORKS BY CHARMIAN LONDON

The Log of the Snark, 1915
Our Hawaii, 1917
The Book of Jack London, 1921

PHOTO CREDITS AND COPYRIGHT

INDEX

Page numbers in italics represent photos.

A

Adventure, 161
aging, 205-6, 240
Alameda Academy, 38
alcohol, 20, 22, 202, 206, 223
American Railway Union, 102
Anderson Ways shipyard, *106-9*, 107
"The Apostate," 30, *30*
Applegarth, Mabel, 59, *59*

Around the World in the Sloop Spray (Slocum), 105, *105*
The Assassination Bureau, Ltd, 174
Australia, 161, 163
Authors' League of America, 217

B

Barry, Viola, *219*
Battle of the Yalu River, *81*
Battle of Veracruz, 235-8
Belmont Academy, 39
Benicia Fish Patrol, 22, 27
Bosworth, Hobart, 212-13, *214*, 215, *215-16*, *218-19*, 221, 225, *225-6*, 227, *230*, 231
boxing, 174, *176*, 177
Burning Daylight, 47

C

California/Oregon carriage journey, 183, 186, *187-9*
The Call of the Wild (films), 68
The Call of the Wild (novel), 68, 70, *70-1*
Cape Horn cruise, 191-7
capitalism, 5, 30, 39, 100
Chaney, William (biological father), 13, 14, 39
The Chechako (film), 227, *227-9*, 229
child labor, 16-17, 30
Children of the Frost, 53
Chinese Exclusion Act, 30
Chinese farming, 198, *198*, 240
Conway, Jack, *220*, 227
Coxey, Jacob, 32, 35

Coxey's Army, 32, *33*, 34, 35, *35*
The Cruise of the Dazzler, 21
The Cruise of the Snark, 105, *133*, *135*, 141-2, *142-3*, *150*, 159, *159*
Cuba, *86*, 87, *98-9*

D

Darbishire, George, *156*
Daughter of the Snows, 68
death of daughter, 174
Debs, Eugene, 102
Dirigo (ship), 191-7, *191-6*, 195-6
"The Dream of Debs," 102, *103*

E

Eames, Roscoe, *106*, *116*, 121, *121*
earthquake, *104*, 108, 110-16, *110-15*
Ecuador, 164, 167, *168-9*
education, 37, 38
Erie County Penitentiary, 35-7

F

films, 211-12, *211-13*, *217*, 218-23, 227. *see also various films*
financial crisis, 32, 138, 198
fires, *104*, 110, 206
fishing, 17, 20
French Frank, *179*

G

Garbutt, Frank A., *214*, 218, 221
Genthe, Arnold, 6
Glen Ellen Ranch, 93, 173-4, *173-4*, *190*, 198, *198-9*, *200-1*, 211, *246*, *248-9*. *see also* Wolf House
The God of His Fathers, 53
"Goliath," 102
Grand Hotel (Santa Rosa), *110*
Great White Fleet, 105-6, *105*
Guadalcanal. *see* Melanesia

H

Harding, Tom, *156*
Hawaii, 122-3, *123-5*, 125-6, *127*, *132*, 240-2, *240-4*
Hearst, William Randolph, 73, *73*

Heinold, Johnny, *20*, 38
Henry (*Snark* crew), 151, *156*
Homestead steel mill, *29*
horseback riding, *88-9*, 91, *91*, 127, *127*, 175, *190*, *200*
The House of Pride, 126
"Housekeeping in the Klondike," 48, *48*
"How I Became a Socialist," 39
Huerta, Victoriano, 234-5
The Human Drift (*That Dead Men Rise Up Never*), 26

I

illness/disease
    appendicitis, 206
    dysentery, 237-8
    fistula, 161, 163
    Hansen's Disease (leprosy), 125, 135
    kidney issues, 206, 240, 245
    rheumatism, 245
    scurvy, 49
    sun exposure, 161
    tropical fevers, 154, 161
    typhoid, 14
immigration, 11, *29*, 30
Indians. *see* Indigenous peoples
Indigenous peoples, 11, 14, *134*, 135, 138, 140-1, *140-1*, *144-6*, *148-9*, 150, 152-3, *152-5*, *158-60*, 161, *162-3*, *168-9*, *212-13*
industrialization, 11
Intercollegiate Socialist Society (ISS), 101
The Iron Heel, 101

J

Jack London and his Daughters (Joan London), 203
Jack London and His Times (Joan London), 203
Jack London Films. *see* films
"To Jack London" (Sterling), 247
Jacobson, Harry, *156*
Japan, 76. *see also* Korea
Jeffries, James J., 176, *176*
John Barleycorn (film), 216, 221, 222-3, *223*
John Barleycorn (novel), 202, 204-5, 205-6
Johnson, Jack, 176, *176*, 177
Johnson, Martin, 122, *129*, *148*, 153, *156-7*, 162, *162*, 164, 195
Jung, Carl Gustav, 243
The Jungle (Sinclair), 101
junks (boats), *74*, 76

KLONDIKE
PROSPECTOR
(1897–1898)

VAGABOND ACROSS
THE UNITED STATES
AND CANADA
(1894)

REPORTER
IN LONDON
(1902)

TRAVEL IN OREGON
AND CALIFORNIA
(1911)

SAILOR IN
SAN FRANCISCO BAY
(1891–1892)

RANCHER IN
THE SONOMA
VALLEY
(1905–1916)

LIVING IN HAWAII
(1907, 1915–1916)

MEXICAN WAR
CORRESPONDENT
(1914)

TRAVEL IN
ECUADOR AND
PANAMA
(1908–1909)

VOYAGE OF THE *SNARK*
IN POLYNESIA AND SAMOA
(1907–1908)

VOYAGE OF
THE *DIRIGO*
(1912)